The ART of ADULTING

LIFE

SKILLS

for

YOUNG

ADULTS

The Ultimate Guide to Money, Career,
Time Management, Mental Health,
and Relationships

IRL PUBLISHING

This book is dedicated to Brittany, Nicholas, and Madison – the adult humans that I sent into the world.
You are my inspiration.

Contents

Introduction

A dulting. Just reading the word might make you nervous. Remember when you had to call the bank and wished you could just text instead? Or the moment you realized that laundry doesn't magically do itself? Trust me, you're not alone. The transition to adulthood can feel like being thrown into the deep end of a pool, except the pool is filled with bills, responsibilities, and an endless to-do list.

Welcome to "The Art of ADULTING: Life Skills for Young Adults". This book is your life raft. It's here to help keep your head above water while learning to swim in the pool of adulthood. We'll tackle time and money management, career development, cooking and cleaning, personal growth, building thriving relationships, and so much more. By the end of this journey, you'll be able to confidently say, "I got this."

Why is this book necessary? Because Adulting doesn't have to be a horror movie. With the right skills and mindset, it can be more like a well-directed drama with the occasional comic relief. We're shifting the narrative from "adulthood is scary" to "adulthood is doable." You'll learn to approach challenges with the mindset that you can handle them. Because guess what? You can.

At IRL Publishing, I strive to tackle topics that affect people **in real life** and in this book I am passionate about helping young adults like you navigate the path to independence. I've raised three self-sufficient adult humans myself, and I'm dedicated to delivering easy-to-follow guidance that anyone can use. Think of me as your guide, here to turn the daunting concept of adulting into an achievable journey.

This book is organized into chapters, each focusing on a specific aspect of adulting. We'll start with money management because, let's face it, without this, the rest is just chaos. Then, we'll move on to career development, offering actionable strategies to help you find and thrive in your chosen field. Cooking and cleaning will no longer be enemies but allies in your quest for a balanced life. Personal growth will be your compass, guiding you through the ups and downs. Next, we'll dive into building and maintaining thriving relationships because no one should go through this journey alone. As you prepare to spread your wings, we'll delve into essential life skills such as transitioning to your own place, understanding the healthcare system, and mastering travel essentials.

At the end of each chapter, you'll find key takeaways. These are little nuggets of wisdom to keep in your back pocket. They'll help reinforce the most critical points, ensuring you can easily remember and apply the advice. Consider them your cheat sheet for adulting.

So, what can you expect from this book? Practical, actionable, and motivational content. This isn't just a book to read; it's a guide to engage with. I encourage you to actively apply the strategies to your own life. Try out the budgeting tips, experiment with the easy recipes, and use the career advice to nail that job interview. Each chapter is designed to empower you with the skills you need to thrive.

In conclusion, this book is your toolkit for adulting. It's filled with humor, support, and empathy because we all need a little laugh and a shoulder to lean on. You're not alone in this journey. Together, we'll navigate the ups and downs, and you'll come out the other side knowing that, yes, you absolutely got this.

So, are you ready to dive in? Let's transform adulting from an overwhelming task into an exciting and manageable adventure. The journey starts now.

Chapter 1

Mastering Your Finances

E ver had that moment at the checkout line where you anxiously swipe your debit card, hoping it doesn't get declined? Yep, we've all been there. Welcome to adulting, where managing your finances can feel overwhelming. But here's the good news: it doesn't have to be that way. This chapter is about turning that financial anxiety into financial confidence. We're going to dig into the nitty-gritty of budgeting, a skill that is so essential it should be taught in high school. But since it wasn't, let's get you up to speed now.

Budgeting 101: Creating a Realistic Budget

Why is budgeting so important? Think of it as the foundation of your financial house. Without a budget, your finances can quickly spiral out of control. A budget is simply a plan for spending your money each month. It helps you track expenses, save money, and avoid debt. Without it, you can't see how much you're spending or what you even have available to spend.

Let's take Sarah for example, a recent college grad who landed her first job. She was so excited to earn her own money, she didn't bother with a budget. Fast-forward a few months, and Sarah wondered where all her money went. Spoiler alert: it went to daily lattes, Lyft rides, and spontaneous online shopping sprees. Sarah's financial stress could have been avoided with a simple budget. According to a study, 67% of young adults without a budget report feeling stressed out by money issues. That's a lot of unnecessary anxiety.

Now, let's get practical. Creating a budget isn't as complicated as it sounds. You start by identifying your income sources. This could be your salary, freelance gigs, or even a side hustle. Once you know how much money is coming in, list your expenses. Split them into fixed expenses that stay the same every month (like rent and car payments) and variable expenses (like food and entertainment). Separating these helps you see where you can cut back if needed.

Consider using budgeting tools and apps like *Mint* or *YNAB* (You Need a Budget) to make budgeting easier. These apps sync with your bank accounts, categorize your spending, and even provide insights on how to improve. With *Mint*, you can set spending limits for different categories and get alerts if you're about to overspend. *YNAB*, on the other hand, uses a zero-based budgeting method, making sure that every dollar you earn is allocated to a specific purpose. Whether paying bills, saving, or spending, you know exactly where your money goes.

Creating a simple budget template can also be helpful. You can use a spreadsheet or even a pen and paper. List your income at the top, followed by your fixed and variable expenses. Subtract your total expenses from your total income, and voilà, you have a budget. If your expenses exceed your income, it's time to see where you can cut back; maybe on dining out or a cheaper phone plan.

Click here for a simple **BUDGET TEMPLATE** that you can use.

Or scan this QR code:

BUDGET

Most people need help with sticking to a budget. The key is to set realistic spending limits. Don't expect to go from spending $200 a month on eating out to $0 overnight. Start small and gradually reduce your spending. Monitoring your budget regularly is important and can help keep you on track. Set aside a few minutes each week or so to review your spending and adjust as needed.

Common budgeting mistakes include overestimating your income, ignoring small expenses, and not accounting for irregular expenses. Overestimating your income can lead to overspending, so always base your budget on your actual take-home pay. Ignoring small expenses, like your daily coffee run, can add up over time. Track every expense, no matter how small. Lastly, account for irregular expenses like car maintenance or annual subscriptions. Setting aside a small amount each month for these expenses can save you from financial surprises.

I know budgeting might seem like a chore, but it's a critical step in taking control of your finances. Creating a realistic budget allows you to track your expenses, save money, and avoid debt. And the best part? You'll finally be able to swipe your card at the checkout line without feeling anxious.

Saving Strategies: Building an Emergency Fund

Imagine you're cruising down the highway, blasting your favorite playlist, when suddenly your car makes a noise that can only be described as a death rattle. You pull over, pop the hood, and realize you'll need a tow and some serious repairs. These are the moments when an emergency fund saves the day. It's your financial safety net, providing peace of mind when life throws you a curveball. According to a survey, almost 40% of Americans would find it difficult to cover an emergency expense of $400. An emergency fund means you won't have to scramble or resort to high-interest credit cards when the unexpected happens.

So, how much should you save in your emergency fund? A good rule of thumb is to have three to six months' worth of living expenses tucked away. This might sound like a lot, but think about it: if you lose your job tomorrow, having a few months' buffer can keep you afloat while you search for new opportunities. Start with short-term goals, like saving $500, then gradually work up to that three-to-six-month cushion. The key is to make it manageable without getting overwhelmed by the end goal.

Building that emergency fund quickly doesn't have to feel like climbing a mountain. Set up an automatic transfer in your banking app so a set amount of your paycheck gets moved into your savings account before you even see it. This "out of sight, out of mind" approach makes saving painless. Another strategy is to cut non-essential expenses. Yes, this might mean fewer Uber Eats orders and more home-cooked meals, but your future self will thank you. Use extra income like tax refunds and work bonuses to boost your savings fund. Instead of splurging on the latest digital device or must-have pair of shoes, consider it an investment in your financial peace of mind.

Where should you stash this emergency fund? High-yield savings accounts are a great option because they offer better interest rates than your regular savings account, helping your money grow faster. Consider using an online bank that offers competitive rates and easy access via a mobile app. This way, your emergency fund is just a few taps away when you need it most. When choosing a high-yield savings account, it's essential to consider not just the best interest rate but these factors as well:

1. Minimum account balance requirements

2. Account fees

3. Ease of access to your funds

In the grand scheme of adulting, an emergency fund is your financial best friend. It's there to catch you when you fall and gives you the confidence to handle life's unexpected twists and turns. By setting aside money now, you're buying yourself peace of mind and financial security. So, start small, make it automatic, and watch your safety net grow.

Credit Scores Unveiled: How to Build and Maintain Good Credit

Alright, let's talk credit scores. Imagine your credit score as your adulting report card. It reflects how responsible you are with borrowed money. This little number can affect everything from renting an apartment to getting a loan for that dream car. A credit score usually ranges from 300 to 850. The higher, the better. It's calculated based on several factors: payment history, credit utilization, length of credit history, types of credit accounts, and recent credit inquiries.

Payment history makes up about 35% of your score. Paying bills on time is super important. Late payments can tank your score faster than you can say "credit card debt." Imagine you're applying for a loan to buy a car. A good score might get you an interest rate of 3%, whereas a poor score could mean a rate as high as 15%. That difference can add up to thousands of dollars over the life of the loan. For fixed expenses like a car payment, or recurring payments such as monthly utilities, set up automatic payments in your banking app. That way the bills are always paid on time and you have less to stress about. Just make sure that you always have enough money in your account to cover the expenses.

Credit utilization, the ratio of your credit card balances to your credit limits, accounts for 30%. Keeping this under 30% is ideal. If you have a $1,000 limit, try not to carry a balance over $300. In fact, try not to carry a balance at all, but if you have to, keep that credit-to-debt ratio low.

So, how do you build good credit from scratch? You can start by opening a secured credit card. This type of card requires a deposit that acts as your credit limit. It's like training wheels for your credit journey. Use it responsibly, making small purchases and paying them off monthly. If you shop regularly at a specific department store or favorite retail store (like Macy's or Target), you can also apply for their credit card, if they have one. These cards start with a lower limit and are usually easier to get approved than a major credit card like VISA or MasterCard. Another option is to become an authorized user on a parent's credit card. This means you get to piggyback on their good credit. Make sure they pay their bills on time, or it could backfire.

Length of credit history accounts for 15% of your score. The longer you've had credit, the better. This is why keeping old accounts open is wise, even if you don't use them much. Types of credit accounts and recent credit inquiries make up the remaining 20%. Having a mix of credit types—like a credit card, student loans, and an auto loan—can boost your score. But don't go overboard applying for new credit. Each inquiry can ding your score slightly.

Maintaining a good credit score is all about consistency. Pay your bills on time, every time. Automate payments if you need to. Keeping your credit utilization low is also vital. Aim to use no more than 30% of your available credit. Regularly check your credit reports for errors. Even small mistakes can have a significant impact. Use free tools like *Credit Karma* to monitor your score and review your report.

Improving your credit score is doable, but it takes time. Start by disputing any errors you find on your credit reports. The major credit bureaus—Equifax, Experian, and TransUnion—are required to investigate disputes. Next, focus on paying down high balances. This can boost your score quickly. And remember, building credit is a marathon, not a sprint.

Now, let's debunk some common credit myths:

- Checking your own credit score lowers it. Nope, checking your score is a soft inquiry and doesn't affect your score.

- Closing old accounts improves your score, right? Wrong again. Keeping old accounts open helps lengthen your credit history.

- Carrying a small balance improves your score. False. It's better to pay off your balance in full each month.

Understanding and managing your credit score is a big part of being in control of your finances. Your credit score is a current picture of your financial health. By following these tips, you'll be well on your way to a stellar credit score, opening doors to better financial opportunities.

Debt Management: Strategies for Paying Off Student Loans and Credit Cards

Debt. Just the word might make you cringe. But let's face it; debt is a reality for many young adults. Whether it's student loans, credit card debt, or personal loans, understanding how to manage it is important. Different types of debt come with their own sets of challenges. Student loans, for example, often have lower interest rates but can linger for decades if not managed properly. On the other hand, credit card debt usually carries higher interest rates, making it easy to get stuck in a cycle of minimum payments and growing balances. Personal loans fall somewhere in between but often come with fixed repayment terms that need careful planning.

Interest rates and repayment terms can feel like a foreign language. Think of interest rates as the cost of borrowing money. The higher the rate, the more you'll pay over time. Repayment terms dictate how long you'll be making payments. For instance, a 30-year student loan might have manageable monthly payments but will cost you more in interest over time. Understanding these elements helps you decide which debts to tackle first.

So, how do you go about paying off debt effectively? Two popular methods are the debt snowball and debt avalanche. The debt snowball method starts with paying off your smallest debts first, giving you quick wins and momentum. The debt avalanche method begins with paying off high interest debts first, saving you money in the long run. Both strategies have their merits, so choose the one that best fits your personality and financial situation.

Consolidation and refinancing are also worth considering. Consolidation involves combining multiple debts into a single loan with one monthly payment, often at a lower interest rate. Refinancing can lower your interest rates on existing loans, reducing your monthly payments and total interest paid. Both options simplify your financial life and can make debt more manageable. Setting up a debt repayment plan is an important first step. List all your debts, their interest rates, and minimum payments. Allocate any extra funds to the debt you're targeting first. Consistency is key here. Make those extra payments religiously and watch your debt shrink.

Avoiding future debt is just as important. The emergency fund we talked about earlier is your financial cushion, which prevents you from using credit cards for unexpected expenses. Practicing mindful spending helps you make intentional purchases, avoiding the temptation to splurge on things you don't need. Use your credit card like a debit card, only spending what you already have in your bank account. If you can't afford it, don't buy it. If you need it, save for it.

Debt isn't just a financial burden; it also takes a psychological toll. The stress and anxiety related to debt can be overwhelming. Sleepless nights, constant worry, and feeling trapped are common. If you find yourself struggling, seeking professional financial counseling can provide relief. Many organizations offer free or low-cost counseling services to help you navigate your debt. Building a supportive network of friends and family who understand your situation can also provide emotional support and encouragement.

Managing credit cards responsibly is a skill that will serve you well. Always pay the balance in full each month to avoid interest charges. Understand the interest rates and fees associated with your card. Some cards offer rewards or cash back, but these perks aren't worth it if you carry a balance and pay high interest. Choose a card that aligns with your spending habits. For example, a travel rewards card might be beneficial if you travel frequently. A low-interest card is better if you're focused on paying off debt.

TIP: If you have a balance on your credit card(s), don't simply make the minimum payment each month—this primarily covers the interest and doesn't make much of a dent in the principal balance. Credit card companies intentionally set the minimum payment low to keep you locked into paying their high interest rates. Strive to pay at least 2x the minimum to ensure that your debt is paid off sooner and with less interest.

In summary, managing debt requires strategy, discipline, and emotional resilience. Whether you're dealing with student loans, credit cards, or personal loans, understanding your options and taking proactive steps can make a world of difference. By employing effective debt repayment methods, avoiding future debt, and managing the psychological impact, you can regain control over your financial life and move towards a debt-free future.

Investing Basics: Your First Steps into the Stock Market

Investing might sound like something reserved for Wall Street big shots. Still, it's actually something everyone should consider, especially if you're looking to grow your wealth over time. You know that feeling when you find a $20 bill in an old pair of jeans? Imagine that times a hundred, and you'll see why investing can be so impactful. Investing is essential for long-term financial health because it allows your money to grow through the magic of compound interest. Compound interest is earning interest on your interest. Think of it as planting a tree and watching it grow more branches and leaves every year. "Compound interest is the eighth wonder of the world. He who understands it earns it; he who doesn't pays it." *-Albert Einstein*

Take the story of Jane, who started investing $100 a month in her mid-twenties. By her mid-forties, her modest monthly investments had grown significantly thanks to compound interest, building a comfortable nest egg. Over the years, those small contributions turned into something substantial, allowing her to make more significant life decisions with financial ease. This isn't a fairy tale; it's the real power of long-term investment growth.

If Jane invested $100 per month for 20 years with compound interest, here's how much she could potentially have, based on different average annual interest rates:

- At 5% interest: $41,103

- At 7% interest: $52,093

- At 10% interest: $75,937

These amounts include the original investments ($24,000) and compound interest growth over time.

Let's break down the different types of investments in simple terms.

- **Stocks** are small pieces of ownership in a company. When you buy a stock, you own a tiny part of that company. Stocks can grow your money faster but also lose value quickly, so they carry more risk.

- **Bonds** are like lending money to a company or the government. In return, they promise to pay you back with interest. Bonds are usually safer than stocks but don't make as much money over time.

- **Mutual Funds** combine money from many people to invest in a mix of stocks, bonds, or other things. This helps spread out risk because you're not putting all your money in one place.

- **ETFs (Exchange-Traded Funds)** are similar to mutual funds but can be bought and sold like individual stocks. They offer the same kind of mix of investments and are usually easier to trade.

When you invest, it's important to consider risk and reward. Higher-risk investments, like stocks, might give you bigger gains but can also be unpredictable. Lower-risk options, like bonds, are more stable but typically offer smaller returns. The goal is to find a balance that matches how much risk you're comfortable with and what you want to achieve financially.

For those with limited funds, starting small with robo-advisors like *Betterment* or *Wealthfront* is smart. These platforms use algorithms to manage your investments affordably, even with minimal starting capital. Investing in fractional shares is another excellent strategy, allowing you to own part of high-priced stocks, such as Amazon or Google, without buying a full share. Automating contributions to your investment accounts can further simplify the process, ensuring consistent savings without the hassle. Key investment strategies include diversification, which involves spreading your investments across various asset classes to mitigate risk.

Investing is not about getting rich quickly; it's about growing your wealth steadily over time. It's about making smart financial decisions today that will benefit you in the future. So, starting is what matters, whether using a robo-advisor, investing in fractional shares, or setting up automatic contributions. You don't need a lot of money to begin investing, just the willingness to take that first step. Remember, the best time to plant a tree was 20 years ago. The second-best time is now.

Key takeaways:

1. Mastering the art of budgeting is essential for ensuring long-term financial stability. Start by tracking your expenses to see where you can cut back and save.

2. Building an emergency fund should be a high priority, aiming for at least three to six months of living expenses.

3. Understanding credit scores, how they are calculated, and their impact can help you make informed decisions about using credit wisely.

4. Managing debt effectively involves knowing the difference between good debt and bad debt and strategies for paying them off efficiently.

5. Lastly, investing is not just for the wealthy; it's a smart way to

grow your savings over time. Consider starting with low-risk investments and gradually diversifying your portfolio.

Chapter 2

Navigating the Job Market

You've just finished school, maybe you've done a few internships, and now you're facing the daunting task of entering the job market. It's like standing at the edge of a cliff, looking down at a swirling sea of LinkedIn profiles, job applications, and interview questions. But don't worry, this chapter is your parachute. We're diving into the details of job hunting, starting with the most significant tool in your arsenal: the resume.

Crafting the Perfect Resume: Templates and Tips

Picture this: you're a hiring manager sifting through a mountain of resumes. Each one is a snapshot of someone's professional life, and you have about six seconds to decide if it's worth a closer look. That's the reality of the job market. A well-crafted resume can make all the difference. It's your first impression, your elevator pitch on paper. It showcases your skills and experiences, setting you apart from the sea of applicants. A strong resume can lead to interviews, and interviews can lead to job offers. Simple, right?

Take the case of Jamie, a recent college grad who landed a dream job at a tech startup. Jamie's resume was a masterpiece. It highlighted relevant skills, showcased impressive achievements, and was tailored to the job description. The hiring manager didn't just see another entry-level candidate; they saw a potential star. Jamie's story isn't unique. A standout resume can open doors you didn't even know existed.

So, what makes a resume stand out? Let's break it down.

- First, you need clear and concise contact information. Your full name, address (at least City/State), email, and phone number should be at the top. And please use a professional email address. "PartyAnimal123" might have been fun in high school, but it won't impress a hiring manager. I recommend using your full name, i.e., janesmith@email.com.

- Next, include an objective statement or summary. This is your chance to tell the employer who you are and what you want. Be specific and keep it short. Something like, "Detail-oriented marketing graduate with a passion for social media strategy, seeking an entry-level position to leverage creative skills and drive brand engagement."

TIP: This is where AI can help. Using a tool like *ChatGPT*, you can ask it to create a summary for you based on the work experience section of your resume.

- Your work experience section should be a highlight reel of your career so far. List your jobs in reverse chronological order, starting with the most recent. Focus on accomplishments rather than duties. Instead of saying, "Responsible for social media posts," say, "Increased social media engagement by 30% through targeted campaigns." Employers want to see stats in your experience showing the value you can bring to the company. Use bullet points to make this section easy to read.

- Remember your education and certifications. Include the names of the schools, degrees earned, and any relevant honors or awards. If you have a high GPA or completed a noteworthy project, mention it. This section is critical for recent graduates with limited work experience.

- Skills and competencies are your chance to show off what makes you unique. Include hard skills (like proficiency in Microsoft Office or Adobe Creative Cloud) and soft skills (like time management and problem-solving). Tailor this section to the job you're applying for. If the job posting mentions specific skills, make sure they appear on your resume.

Tailoring your resume for specific jobs is key. One size does NOT fit all. Start by carefully analyzing the job description. Highlight relevant skills and experiences that match the job requirements. Use keywords from the job listing. Many companies use applicant tracking systems (ATS) to scan resumes for these keywords. If your resume doesn't include them, a human might not even see it.

> **TIP:** Again, this is where AI can help. Copy and paste in your work experience and ask *ChatGPT* to rewrite it to make it relevant to a specific job description, and then paste in the job description. Copy/paste the results back into your resume and make any necessary adjustments.

A cover letter complements your resume so you can showcase your personality. Personalize each cover letter for the job you're applying to. Address it to a specific person if possible. Structure it with a strong introduction, a compelling body, and a confident conclusion. Demonstrate your knowledge of the company and explain why you're a perfect fit for the role. Share a brief story or example that highlights your qualifications.

If you're applying to jobs listed on LinkedIn and the listing includes the name of the hiring manager or recruiter, reach out to them. Ask them to connect with you and send a message introducing yourself. This will help you stand out among the other applicants pre-screened by the ATS software.

Common resume mistakes can be deal-breakers. Overloading your resume with unnecessary information can make it hard to read. Stick to relevant details. Using an unprofessional email address is a rookie mistake. Including irrelevant job experiences can dilute your message. Focus on what's pertinent to the job you want.

To wrap up:

1. Remember that your resume is a living document; keep it updated. You never know when you'll need it.

2. Be sure to tailor it for each job application and include relevant keywords.

3. Proofread thoroughly to avoid typos and grammatical errors.

4. Use active language and action verbs like "achieved," "led," and "created."

Your resume is your ticket to that dream job, so make it count.
Click here for a well-formatted RESUME TEMPLATE.
Or scan this QR code:

Acing the Interview: Common Questions and Best Practices

So, you've crafted the perfect resume, and now you've landed an interview. Cue the sweaty palms and racing heart. Interviews can be nerve-wracking, but you can turn that anxiety into confidence with preparation. Think of it like studying for a big exam. The more you prepare, the better you'll perform. Interview preparation is critical not just for your confidence but also for making a great impression. A well-prepared candidate stands out, demonstrating that they're serious about the position and have taken the time to understand the company and the role.

Take the story of Alex, who spent hours researching the company, practicing answers to common questions, and even rehearsing in front of the mirror. When Alex walked into the interview, it was clear they were ready. The preparation paid off, and Alex got the job. Preparation reduces anxiety because you're not walking into the interview blind. It builds confidence because you know you've done everything possible to present yourself in the best light.

Now, let's talk about those common interview questions. One of the most frequently asked questions is, "Tell me about yourself." This isn't an invitation to narrate your life story. Instead, focus on your professional background and how it relates to the job. Use the present, past, and future format:

- Discuss your current role or status.

- Touch on relevant past experiences.

- Explain how this role fits into your future goals.

Another classic is, "What are your strengths and weaknesses?" For strengths, pick skills relevant to the job and provide examples. For weaknesses, choose something genuine, but not critical to the role you're interviewing for, and explain how you're working to improve it. Tailor your answers to align with the job description. If the job requires strong teamwork skills, highlight your collaborative experiences. If it emphasizes problem-solving, share a story where you solved a challenging issue.

The STAR method (Situation, Task, Action, Result) is your best friend for behavioral questions. Let's break it down.

- **Situation**: Explain the circumstances or environment in which you completed a task or encountered a challenge.

- **Task**: Explain the actual task or challenge involved.

- **Action**: Detail your specific actions to address the task or challenge.

- **Result**: Share the outcomes of your actions.

For example, if asked, "Tell me about a time when you faced a tight deadline," you could say: "In my previous job, we had a project due in two weeks (Situation). I was responsible for coordinating the team's efforts (Task). I organized daily check-ins and set mini-deadlines to track progress (Action). We finished the project on time and received positive feedback from the client (Result)."

TIP: Above are examples of general interview questions. To prepare for the questions specific to the role you are interviewing for, ask *Chat-GPT* to list the top 10-15 interview questions for that specific job title. You can even paste in the job description if you feel the results are not specific enough. Format your answers to these questions in the STAR format, then study, study, study and nail that interview.

Virtual interviews are now a staple in the job application process, presenting unique challenges. Create a distraction-free, professional backdrop with optimal lighting—preferably natural, or use a lamp to illuminate your face evenly. Before the interview, check your tech essentials: stable internet, functional webcam, and clear microphone. During the interview, direct your gaze at the camera instead of the screen to foster a sense of engagement and connection.

Non-verbal communication is just as important as what you say. Your body language should convey confidence and professionalism. Dress appropriately for the company culture. If you're unsure, it's better to be slightly overdressed than underdressed. Arrive on time, ideally a few minutes early. A firm handshake sets a positive tone, and maintaining eye contact shows engagement. Keep a confident posture; sit up straight and avoid fidgeting. These small details can leave a lasting impression.

After the interview, proactively follow up by sending a thank-you email within 24 hours. In this email, thank the interviewer for the opportunity, reaffirm your interest in the position, and reference a specific moment from the interview that underscores your suitability for the role. This demonstrates professionalism and ensures you remain memorable. If there are any points you wish to clarify or expand upon from the interview, this email is your opportunity to do so.

Interviews are a critical part of the job search process. While they can be stressful, thorough preparation can make a world of difference. Understanding common questions, practicing your answers, mastering your non-verbal cues, and following up can turn that nerve-wracking experience into a successful step toward your dream job.

Job Offers: Negotiating the Pay & Benefits You Deserve

You've aced the interview and are now staring at a job offer in your inbox. Congratulations! But before planning how to spend your first paycheck, you must evaluate the offer thoroughly. It's more than just looking at the salary number and saying, "Yup, that'll do." There are multiple factors to consider that will affect your overall happiness and satisfaction in the role.

First, let's talk about salary and benefits. The salary is the obvious part—it's the number that will show up in your bank account. However, don't just focus on the base salary. Look at the entire compensation package. Does it include bonuses, stock options, or other financial perks? Health insurance can be a significant expense if your employer doesn't cover it. Check what kind of health plans they offer, including dental and vision. Retirement plans like a 401(k) or pension are important for long-term financial health. Some companies offer employer matching for your contributions, basically free money for your future. Paid time off (PTO) is another significant benefit. How much vacation time do you get? Other perks might include gym memberships, tuition reimbursement, or wellness programs. These can add value to your overall compensation package.

Work-life balance is another critical factor. A high salary might not be worth it if you're expected to work 60-hour weeks with no flexibility. Ask about remote work options, flexible hours, and the company's stance on overtime. Company culture and values are often overlooked but can make or break your job satisfaction. Research the company's work environment, read employee reviews, and try to gauge if their values align with yours. A supportive, inclusive culture can significantly enhance your work experience.

Once you've looked over the offer, it's time to negotiate. Yes, negotiate. The first offer is rarely the best, and you don't want to leave money on the table. Start by researching industry salary standards for the role you're considering. Websites like *Glassdoor* and *Payscale* can give you ballpark numbers. Knowing the industry benchmarks will give you confidence in your negotiations. Prepare and practice your negotiation conversation. Write down your talking points and rehearse them. You want to be clear, concise, and confident. Remember, you're negotiating your worth, so don't sell yourself short.

When preparing a counteroffer, be reasonable but assertive. If the offered salary is $50,000 and you aim for $55,000 based on your research, that's a fair counter. Frame your request by highlighting your value and achievements. For example, you could say, "Given my extensive experience in project management and my track record of delivering projects on time, I believe a salary of $55,000 would align with my qualifications." This shows that your request is based on merit, not just a desire for more money.

Negotiating your job offer might seem intimidating (I can still remember the first time I did it, whew), but it's necessary to secure the pay and benefits you deserve. No one else is going to advocate for you. By evaluating all aspects of the offer, confidently negotiating your salary, and understanding the importance of benefits packages, you can make an informed decision that sets you up for success. Remember, you're not just accepting a job but setting the foundation for your future career. So, take the time to make sure everything aligns with your goals and values.

Accepting or declining a job offer is a big decision, and it's okay to seek advice. Talk to mentors, trusted friends, or family members who can provide an objective perspective. Once you've made your decision, communicate it professionally. If you're accepting, a simple but gracious email will do. If you're declining, thank the employer for the opportunity and express your regret. Keep the door open for future possibilities; you never know when paths might cross again.

Optimizing Your LinkedIn Profile: Stand Out Online

LinkedIn has become the preferred platform for recruiters and jobseekers alike. Imagine your LinkedIn profile as your digital handshake—it's your first impression on potential employers. A well-optimized profile can be the key to unlocking job opportunities you didn't even know existed. Recruiters often use LinkedIn to find candidates before positions are even posted online. In fact, many recruiters rely heavily on LinkedIn to source talent, making it vital for you to have a polished presence on the platform.

Take, for example, the story of Maria, a recent college graduate who landed a job at a top marketing firm. Her LinkedIn profile was a standout, featuring a professional photo, a compelling headline, and a detailed summary. Recruiters were drawn to her profile because it was clear, concise, and effectively showcased her skills and accomplishments. Maria's success isn't isolated; countless professionals have secured job offers through a well-crafted LinkedIn profile.

So, what are the key sections of a LinkedIn profile that you need to focus on? Let's start with the professional photo. This isn't the time for selfies or photos from your last beach vacation. A clear, high-quality headshot with a neutral background works best. Your image should be professional but approachable. Don't be afraid to smile. Think of it as your digital first impression.

Next, you need a compelling headline. This line appears right below your name and is one of the first things people see. Instead of just listing your job title, use this space to showcase your skills and what you bring to the table. For example, "Creative Marketing Specialist | Expert in Social Media Strategy & Content Creation" is far more engaging than just "Marketing Specialist."

Your detailed summary is your elevator pitch. Use this section to tell your story. Highlight your career achievements, skills, and what you're passionate about. Keep it concise but informative. Use bullet points to break up the text and make it easier to read. Include keywords relevant to your industry to improve your searchability. Think of this as the narrative that connects all the dots on your resume.

When it comes to work experience, follow the same format that we covered for your resume. Instead of saying, "Managed social media accounts," say, "Increased social media engagement by 30% through targeted campaigns." Numbers and specific achievements make your experience more compelling and credible. Recruiters want to see what impact you've made in your previous roles.

Skills endorsements and recommendations are indispensable. List skills that are relevant to your field and get endorsements from colleagues and supervisors. Recommendations add a layer of credibility to your profile. Reach out to former bosses or coworkers and ask for a brief recommendation. Ask them to tailor the recommendation to the skills that you are trying to highlight. Asking may feel a little awkward but it's totally worth it.

Using LinkedIn for job hunting involves more than just having a polished profile. Set up job alerts to be notified when positions matching your criteria are posted. Apply directly through LinkedIn to streamline the application process. The "Open to Work" feature is a great way to signal recruiters that you're actively seeking opportunities. It increases your visibility and makes it easier for recruiters to find you.

Let's not forget the power of a well-crafted LinkedIn profile in making connections. Think of LinkedIn as a digital networking event. The more you engage, the more visible you become. Share your thoughts on trends, comment on industry news, and don't hesitate to reach out to professionals you admire. A simple message like, "I enjoyed your recent article on digital marketing trends and would love to connect," can go a long way.

Your LinkedIn profile is more than just a digital resume. It's a dynamic platform where you can showcase your skills, engage with industry professionals, and actively search for job opportunities. By optimizing each section of your profile, leveraging LinkedIn's job search features, and building a robust network, you can significantly enhance your job search efforts.

As we wrap up Chapter 2, remember that navigating the job market is more than just having a strong resume and acing interviews. It's about leveraging all the tools at your disposal, including a well-optimized LinkedIn profile, to stand out and connect with the right opportunities. Now, let's move forward with the confidence that you have the tools and knowledge to make your mark in the professional world.

Key takeaways:

1. In today's competitive job market, your first impressions are a standout resume and a strong LinkedIn profile.

2. Tailor your resume to each job application, highlighting relevant skills and experiences.

3. Preparing for interviews is crucial; research common interview questions and practice your responses.

4. Don't underestimate the power of negotiation; understanding your value and the market rate for your role can significantly affect your starting salary and benefits.

5. Continuous networking and upskilling can also pave the way for future opportunities.

Chapter 3

Mastering Time Management and Organization

Have you ever looked at your to-do list and felt like you needed a nap just from reading it? Welcome to the chaos of modern life, where balancing work, school, social activities, and self-care feels like a juggling act. But here's the thing: time is the one resource we all have in equal measure, and how you manage it can make or break your day. This chapter guides you to wrangling that wild beast called "time."

Mastering Time: Tools and Techniques for Effective Time Management

Time management isn't about squeezing more hours into the day. It's about managing your activities within the time you have. Think of it as getting the most bang for your buck, except the currency is hours, not dollars. Effective time management can skyrocket your productivity, reduce stress, and give you more free time to binge-watch your favorite shows guilt-free. Who doesn't want that?

According to the University of Georgia, good time management can lead to better relationships and improved self-esteem. So, what exactly is time management? It's organizing and planning how to divide your time between specific activities. Good time management enables you to work smarter, not harder, ensuring you get more done in less time—even when time is tight and pressures are high.

Now, let's explore some popular time management techniques that can help you reclaim your time.

- First up is the **Pomodoro Technique**, which involves working for 25 minutes and then taking a 5-minute break. After four sessions, take an extended break of 15-30 minutes. It's like interval training for your brain. The idea is to keep your mind fresh and focused, preventing burnout and improving productivity. Apps like *Focus Booster* can help you stick to these intervals.

- Another effective method is **Time Blocking**. This involves scheduling specific blocks of time for different tasks or activities. Imagine your day as a giant Tetris game, where each block represents a task. By assigning a specific time slot for each activity, you can focus solely on one task without distractions. *Google Calendar* is excellent for this. You can color-code tasks, set reminders, and even integrate it with other tools like *Asana* for a seamless experience.

- The **Two-Minute Rule** is perfect for tackling those tiny tasks that often get overlooked. If a task takes less than two minutes, do it immediately. This could be anything from replying to an email to putting away laundry. It's a great way to prevent small tasks from piling up and becoming overwhelming. This rule is particularly useful for procrastinators, making starting a task less daunting.

Speaking of tools, let's talk about how to implement these time management techniques using various apps.

- **Digital calendars** like *Google Calendar* are lifesavers. They sync across all your devices, ensuring you never miss an appointment or deadline. You can also set recurring events and use color coding to differentiate between work, personal, and social activities.

- **Time-tracking** apps like *Toggl* can help you understand where your time goes. By tracking your activities, you can identify time-wasting habits and make adjustments. *Toggl* is particularly useful for freelancers or anyone who bills by the hour. It provides detailed reports, helping you see how much time you spend on each task.

- **Task management** apps like *Trello* and *Asana* are fantastic for organizing your to-dos. *Trello* uses boards, lists, and cards to help you manage projects and tasks visually. It's great for both personal use and team collaboration. *Asana* offers more advanced features like timelines and workload management, making it ideal for more complex projects.

Of course, even the best tools and techniques can't eliminate common time management challenges. Procrastination is a big one. It's easy to put off tasks, especially if they're unpleasant. One trick is to tackle the hardest task first thing in the morning, a strategy known as "eating the frog." Gross. But once that's out of the way, everything else is easy peasy.

Multitasking might seem like a good idea, but it often reduces productivity and increases errors. Focus on one task at a time to improve efficiency and quality. If you find yourself constantly switching between tasks, try allocating specific times for checking emails or social media and stick to those times.

Interruptions and distractions are inevitable, but you can manage them. Set boundaries by creating a dedicated workspace and letting others know when you're not to be disturbed. Use noise-canceling headphones or play background music to drown out distractions. If interruptions are a significant issue, consider using apps like *StayFocusd* to block distracting websites.

So there you have it. Time management is all about making the most of the hours you have. You can turn chaos into order by mastering techniques like the Pomodoro Technique, time blocking, and the Two-Minute Rule, as well as using tools like *Google Calendar*, *Toggl*, and *Trello*. Remember, the goal isn't to do more but to do what matters most efficiently. Now, let's get to it!

Prioritizing Tasks: Setting Realistic Goals

Ever feel like your to-do list is plotting against you? No matter how much you cross off, does it somehow grow longer? Welcome to the world of task prioritization. Setting priorities isn't just about picking what to do first; it's about creating clarity and focus. You know what needs to be done, when it needs to be done, and why it's important. This clarity reduces stress and increases productivity. On the flip side, failing to prioritize can lead to missed deadlines, forgotten tasks, and a constant feeling of being overwhelmed. Think of it as trying to juggle without knowing which ball to catch first—you're bound to drop a few.

Different prioritization methods can help you tackle your to-do list with ninja-like precision.

- The **Eisenhower Matrix** involves sorting tasks into four quadrants: urgent and important, important but not urgent, urgent but not important, and neither urgent nor important. Urgent tasks have a looming deadline and important tasks—well, they're important. By focusing on what's urgent and important, you make sure critical tasks get done first.

- Next up is the **ABCDE Method**. This involves labeling tasks with letters: A for must-do tasks, B for should-do tasks, and so on. It's a simple yet effective way to rank tasks by importance.

- Then there's the **MoSCoW Method**, which stands for Must have, Should have, Could have, and Won't have. This method helps you prioritize tasks based on necessity and desirability, making it easier to focus on what truly matters.

Setting realistic goals is vital for turning your priorities into actionable steps. One effective approach is using SMART criteria. SMART stands for Specific, Measurable, Achievable, Relevant, and Time-bound. For example, instead of saying, "I want to exercise more," a SMART goal would be, "I will run three times a week for 30 minutes each time over the next month." This goal is clear, measurable, and has a deadline, making it more achievable. Breaking down large goals into smaller, manageable tasks can also make them less overwhelming. If your goal is to write a research paper, break it down into tasks like researching, outlining, drafting, and revising. Each smaller task feels more manageable, and you'll progress steadily toward your larger goal.

Life, however, loves to throw curveballs, so staying flexible is key. Regularly reassessing your goals allows you to adjust your priorities as circumstances change. Maybe a new project comes up at work, or you encounter unexpected challenges. Being open to change and adaptability helps you stay on track without feeling frustrated. Managing unexpected tasks and emergencies requires a bit of juggling, but it's doable. Keep a buffer in your schedule for last-minute changes, and don't be afraid to reprioritize tasks when necessary. It's about balancing between sticking to your plan and being flexible enough to handle the unexpected.

Reflection Exercise

1. **List Your Top 5 Goals**: Write down the five most important goals you want to achieve in the next month.

2. **Prioritize Using a Method**: Choose one of the prioritization methods mentioned—Eisenhower Matrix, ABCDE, or MoSCoW—and categorize your goals.

3. **Set SMART Criteria**: Write a SMART version for each goal to make it clear and actionable.

4. **Break Down Large Goals**: Break down any large goals into smaller tasks. List these tasks under each goal.

5. **Review and Adjust Weekly**: At the end of each week, revisit your list. Reassess and adjust as needed based on any new priorities or changes.

By setting clear priorities and realistic goals, you'll get more done and feel more in control of your time and energy. This approach reduces stress and increases your sense of accomplishment. So, grab that to-do list and start prioritizing like a pro.

Using Planners and To-Do Lists: Staying on Track

Feeling overwhelmed is like having a browser with too many open tabs. Planners and to-do lists act as a navigational tool, organizing your tasks and reducing mental clutter. Visualization aids in planning and prevents last-minute scrambles, offering a satisfying sense of accomplishment as tasks are completed.

Utilizing planners has been proven to enhance productivity and decrease stress. They serve as an external memory for deadlines and personal reminders, allowing you to focus on one task at a time. The choice between digital and paper planners depends on personal preference. Digital versions offer convenience and synchronization across devices. At the same time, paper planners provide a tactile experience without the worry of battery life.

Selecting a planner should be based on your needs. Some feature sections for notes and goals, while others focus on tasks and deadlines. Planners with goal-setting spaces can be beneficial for goal-oriented individuals. The important thing is to choose a tool that will be consistently used and enjoyed.

Effective to-do lists require prioritization and specificity. Tasks should be actionable and broken down into smaller, manageable parts for easier execution. Consistency in updating and reviewing these lists is key to staying organized and should become as routine as daily hygiene.

In essence, planners and to-do lists are life's roadmaps, guiding you toward your goals through the chaos of daily responsibilities. Whether digital or paper, the right tool can significantly enhance your organizational skills, leading to a more productive and stress-free life.

Digital Tools for Organization: Apps and Software Recommendations

Imagine trying to juggle your daily tasks, appointments, and deadlines without some digital assistance. It's like trying to cook a three-course meal without a recipe—pretty chaotic. Digital tools can be your sous-chefs, making organization more accessible and more efficient. One of the biggest perks of digital tools is their accessibility and convenience. Whether you're on your laptop, tablet, or phone, you can access your schedule, to-do lists, and notes from anywhere. This means no more scrambling to remember what you had planned for the day or where you wrote down that important piece of information.

Integration with other digital platforms is another advantage. Many apps sync with your email, calendar, and even other task management tools, creating a seamless ecosystem where everything works together. For instance, *Google Calendar* can integrate with *Trello*, allowing you to see your tasks and deadlines in one place. Real-life examples show how digital tools can streamline your life. Take Jamie, a college student balancing part-time work and classes. By using *Todoist* for task tracking and *Google Calendar* for scheduling, Jamie managed to stay on top of assignments and work shifts without breaking a sweat.

Let's dive into some recommended apps.

- *Todoist* is a fantastic app for task tracking. It offers natural language input, so you can type tasks like "Submit report by Friday," and it will automatically set the due date. You can also create projects, set priorities, and track your productivity with built-in reports.

- *Trello*, which we discussed earlier, is perfect for project management. It uses boards, lists, and cards to help you visualize your tasks. Whether you're planning a group project or organizing a solo venture, *Trello's* drag-and-drop interface makes it intuitive and flexible.

- *Microsoft To Do* is a solid choice for those who prefer simplicity. It's great for making simple lists and setting reminders. You can categorize tasks into lists, set due dates, and add subtasks. Its interface is clean and uncluttered, making it easy to use without overwhelming you with features.

These apps cater to different needs, so you can choose the one that fits your style.

Incorporating these digital tools into your daily routine can transform how you manage your tasks and time. They provide the structure and support you need to stay organized, reduce stress, and enhance productivity. So, try these apps and see how they can help you streamline your life.

Maintaining Work-Life Balance: Strategies for Setting Boundaries

Finding the balance between work and personal life can feel like walking a tightrope. One wrong move, and you're plunging into a sea of burnout and stress. Achieving a balance is not just a nice to have; it's necessary for your well-being. Avoiding burnout and stress means you'll have more energy and enthusiasm for work and play. The overall quality of your life improves when you're not constantly worrying about work or feeling overwhelmed by personal obligations.

Setting clear boundaries between work and personal time is your first step towards this nirvana. Resist the urge to check emails or finish that "one last thing." The occasional staying a little late to meet a critical deadline is understandable, but make this the exception, not the norm. Creating a dedicated workspace can also help. Whether it's a home office or a corner of your room, having a specific place for work can mentally separate work time from personal time. Communicating these boundaries with colleagues and family is necessary. Let them know your work hours and when you're available for personal interactions. Your roommate shouldn't ask about dinner plans while you're on a Zoom call, and your boss needs to know you're off the grid after hours.

Incorporating self-care into your daily routine is not just a luxury; it's a necessity. Schedule regular breaks and downtime throughout your day.

This could be a quick walk, a coffee break, or even a few minutes of deep breathing. Practicing mindfulness and relaxation techniques can also support your work-life balance. More about that in the next chapter. Another form of self-care is engaging in hobbies and activities that bring you joy. Whether it's painting, gardening, or playing video games, make time for activities that recharge your batteries.

Remote work presents its own set of challenges. Without the physical separation of an office, it's easy for work to bleed into personal time. Setting up a productive home office is key. Choose a spot that's quiet, well-lit, and free of distractions. Establishing a clear work routine can also help. Start and end your workday at the same time every day, and take regular breaks just as you would in a traditional office. Staying connected with colleagues virtually is essential, too. Use tools like *Slack* or *Microsoft Teams* to keep in touch and maintain a sense of camaraderie. Virtual coffee breaks or team-building activities can make remote work feel less isolating.

Maintaining work-life balance is a continuous process that requires effort and commitment. By setting clear boundaries, incorporating self-care into your routine, and addressing the unique challenges of remote work, you can achieve a healthier, more balanced life. Remember, it's not about working harder; it's about working smarter and taking care of yourself in the process.

Key takeaways:

1. Adopting time management techniques can transform your productivity.

2. The Pomodoro Technique, for instance, involves working in focused intervals with short breaks to boost efficiency.

3. Time blocking helps allocate specific blocks of time for tasks, minimizing distractions.

4. The Eisenhower Matrix helps prioritize tasks based on urgency and importance, ensuring that you focus on what truly matters.

Chapter 4

Prioritizing Mental Health and Stress Management

Picture this: you're sitting at your desk, a mountain of tasks staring back at you, and your mind is racing faster than a squirrel on Redbull. Stress isn't just knocking at your door; it's kicked it down and made itself at home. In a world where we're constantly bombarded with deadlines, notifications, and the pressure to "have it all together," prioritizing mental health isn't just a luxury—it's a necessity. This chapter is about equipping you with the tools to manage stress and your mental well-being, starting with the magic of mindfulness.

Daily Mindfulness Practices: Simple Techniques for Inner Peace

Mindfulness might sound like one of those trendy buzzwords, but it's a game-changer for managing stress and improving overall well-being. Imagine hitting the pause button on your racing thoughts and focusing on the present moment. Studies have shown that mindfulness can significantly reduce anxiety and depression, lower blood pressure, and improve sleep. It even helps people cope with chronic pain. According to the NIH (National Institutes of Health), mindfulness involves focusing on the present moment and observing thoughts, feelings, sensations, and the environment without judgment.

Take Jenna, a college student juggling classes, a part-time job, and a social life. She started practicing mindfulness to manage her stress. By incorporating simple breathing exercises and mindful walking into her daily routine, she noticed a significant reduction in her anxiety levels. Jenna's grades improved, she felt more focused, and she even slept better. Mindfulness is for anyone looking to bring a little more calm into their daily life.

So, how can you incorporate mindfulness into your daily routine without feeling like you need to book a retreat in Bali? Start with some simple exercises that you can practice anywhere.

- One technique is the **4-7-8 breathing exercise**. It's easy: inhale through your nose for a count of four, hold your breath for seven seconds, and then exhale through your mouth for a count of eight. Repeat this a few times, and you'll feel an instant sense of calm washing over you.

- Another effective practice is the **body scan meditation**. This requires lying down or sitting comfortably and mentally scanning your body from head to toe. Focus on how each part of your body feels, releasing any tension you might be holding. It's like giving your muscles a mental massage.

- **Mindful walking** is also incredibly grounding. As you walk, pay attention to the sensation of your feet touching the ground, the flow of your breath, and the surrounding sights and sounds. It's a great way to turn a mundane activity into a moment of mindfulness.

Creating a mindfulness routine doesn't have to be complicated. Set aside specific times for mindfulness, whether it's in the morning to begin your day with tranquility or in the evening to relax and de-stress. You can even incorporate mindfulness into daily activities, like eating or brushing your teeth. Plenty of mindfulness apps like *Insight Timer* and *Smiling Mind* offer guided meditations and exercises to help you get started. Creating a peaceful environment for practice can enhance your mindfulness sessions. Find a quiet corner, light a candle, or play some soothing music. The key is to create a space to relax and focus without distractions.

Of course, practicing mindfulness isn't always smooth sailing. Life gets busy, and it's easy to push mindfulness to the bottom of your to-do list. One common barrier is dealing with a busy schedule. If you're constantly on the go, try integrating mindfulness into activities you already do. For example, practice mindful breathing while waiting in line or do a quick body scan before bed. Managing distractions is another challenge. Our phones are buzzing, emails are pinging, and finding a moment of peace is hard. Set boundaries by turning off notifications during your mindfulness practice. Remind yourself that this is your time to focus and recharge.

Staying motivated can also be tough, especially when you don't see immediate results. Remember that mindfulness is a practice, not a quick fix. Start small; even a few minutes a day can make a difference. Celebrate the small wins, like feeling more relaxed or noticing decreased stress levels. Keep a journal to track your progress and reflect on how mindfulness impacts your life.

Creating a mindfulness routine and overcoming common barriers will help you stay consistent and reap the benefits of this powerful practice. So take a deep breath, embrace the present moment, and let mindfulness be your anchor.

Stress Management Strategies: Practical Solutions for Everyday Stress

Life can sometimes feel like an endless ride on a rollercoaster. While a bit of excitement is great, too much can leave you feeling dizzy and overwhelmed. Stress is a part of life, but when it becomes chronic, it can wreak havoc on your mental and physical health. The first step in managing stress is identifying its sources. For many, work or school pressures top the list. Whether it's meeting tight deadlines, handling a heavy course load, or dealing with demanding bosses or professors, these pressures can create a constant undercurrent of stress.

Financial concerns are another major source of stress. From paying off student loans to managing daily expenses, worrying about money can keep you up at night. Then, there are relationship issues, ranging from conflicts with friends or family to romantic troubles. Navigating these complexities can feel like balancing on a tightrope, and the stress can be palpable.

Once you've pinpointed the sources of your stress, the next step is to tackle them head-on with effective stress management techniques. Exercise and physical activity are fantastic stress busters. Physical activity releases endorphins, which are natural mood lifters. Whether it's a brisk walk, a session at the gym, or a yoga class, moving your body can help clear your mind and reduce stress. Creative outlets like journaling or art can also be incredibly therapeutic. Writing down your thoughts or expressing yourself through art can provide a release for pent-up emotions and help you process your feelings.

Incorporating relaxation techniques into your daily routine can make a significant difference. Progressive muscle relaxation (PMR) involves tensing and then slowly releasing each muscle group in your body, starting from your toes and working your way up. This technique helps reduce physical tension and promote relaxation.

Here's a step-by-step guide on how to perform PMR:

1. Find a quiet and comfortable place:

   ○ Sit or lie down in a comfortable position, ensuring your body is fully supported.

   ○ Close your eyes and take a few deep breaths to settle in.

2. Focus on your breathing:

   ○ Start by taking deep, slow breaths.

   ○ Breathe in through your nose, filling your lungs completely, then exhale slowly through your mouth.

   ○ Focus on your breath to begin calming your mind.

3. Tense and relax each muscle group:

   ○ Starting from either the head or feet, tense one muscle group at a time, hold the tension for 5-10 seconds, then release it gradually and completely.

   ○ Notice the difference between how tension feels and the relaxation that follows.

   ○ **Note:** Be careful not to over-tense or strain muscles, especially if you have any injuries or health concerns.

4. Progress through the following muscle groups:

   ○ Forehead: Raise your eyebrows as high as possible, creating tension in your forehead. Relax.

   ○ Eyes and cheeks: Squeeze your eyes shut tightly and clench your jaw. Relax.

○ Neck and shoulders: Shrug your shoulders up to your ears and hold. Relax.

○ Arms and hands: Clench your fists, tighten your arms, and then release.

○ Chest and upper back: Take a deep breath and hold it, tightening your chest. Relax as you exhale.

○ Stomach: Tighten your abdominal muscles as if bracing for a punch. Relax.

○ Thighs: Squeeze your thighs together tightly. Relax.

○ Lower legs and feet: Point your toes down to tense the calves and feet. Relax.

5. Move through the body progressively:

○ Repeat the tensing and relaxing for each muscle group, moving systematically from one area to the next. This helps to gradually release tension throughout the entire body.

6. Enjoy the state of relaxation:

○ After completing the cycle of tensing and relaxing all muscle groups, take a moment to notice how relaxed your body feels.

○ Continue to breathe slowly and deeply for a few more minutes.

7. End the session gradually:

○ When ready, gently stretch your muscles, open your eyes, and slowly bring your awareness back to the room.

Regular practice of PMR reduces stress and anxiety, improves sleep quality, enhances body awareness, helps manage pain and tension, and promotes a sense of calm.

Visualization techniques can also be beneficial. Close your eyes and imagine a peaceful scene, like a tranquil beach or a peaceful forest. Focus on the sensory details—the sound of the waves, the smell of the pine trees, the feeling of the sand beneath your feet. This mental escape can help you relax and take your mind off your worries.

Monitoring your stress levels is important for maintaining your well-being. Keeping a stress journal can help you track your stressors and identify patterns. Write down what caused your stress, how you felt, and how you responded. Over time, you'll gain insights into what triggers your stress and how to manage it more effectively. Recognizing the signs of chronic stress is also essential. Symptoms can include persistent headaches, fatigue, irritability, and difficulty sleeping. If you notice these signs, it's time to take action.

Despite our best efforts, sometimes stress can become too much to handle alone. Consulting a mental health professional can provide valuable support. Therapists and counselors are trained to help you develop coping strategies and work through your stressors. They can offer a fresh perspective and guide you towards healthier stress management methods.

Stress is an inevitable part of life, but it doesn't have to control you. By identifying your stressors and employing effective management techniques, you can reduce their impact on your life. Incorporating relaxation practices and monitoring your stress levels can help you stay balanced and resilient. And remember, seek professional support if you need to. You're not alone in this, and resources are available to help you navigate the challenges of stress.

Overcoming Anxiety: Practical Strategies for Managing Fear and Worry

Anxiety can feel like a constant, unwelcome companion. It's there when you're trying to concentrate on a work project, when you're meeting new people, or even when you're just trying to fall asleep. Recognizing what triggers your anxiety is the first step in managing it. Common triggers include social situations, where the fear of judgment or rejection can loom large, and work pressure, with tight deadlines and high expectations. Financial worries and relationship issues also rank high on the anxiety-inducing list. Keeping a journal to document these triggers can be incredibly enlightening. Write down when you feel anxious, what you are doing, and what thoughts are running through your mind. Over time, patterns will emerge, giving you insight into what sets off your anxiety and how to anticipate and manage it.

Cognitive Behavioral Therapy (CBT) offers practical strategies for managing anxious thoughts. One powerful technique is challenging negative thoughts. When an anxious thought pops up, ask yourself if it's based on facts or a worst-case scenario your mind has conjured up. Replace these negative thoughts with positive affirmations. For example, if you find yourself thinking, "I'm going to mess up this presentation," replace it with, "I am prepared and capable." Exposure therapy is another effective CBT method, where you gradually face your fears in a controlled way. Start with less intimidating situations and work your way up. This gradual exposure helps desensitize you to the anxiety trigger, making it less scary over time.

When anxiety does strike, sometimes you need quick relief. Breathing and relaxation exercises can provide immediate calm.

- The 4-7-8 breathing technique, that we discussed earlier, is a go-to strategy: inhale through your nose for four seconds, hold for seven, and exhale through your mouth for eight. This method helps slow your heart rate and promote relaxation.

- Box breathing is another effective technique. Inhale for four seconds, hold for four, exhale for four, and hold again for four. Repeat this cycle a few times to help lower your anxiety levels.

Grounding exercises can also be incredibly helpful.

- The 5-4-3-2-1 technique is simple: Identify 5 things you can see, 4 things you can touch, 3 things you can hear, 2 things you can smell, and 1 thing you can taste. This exercise helps you focus back on the present moment, reducing the power of anxious thoughts.

There are times when managing anxiety on your own isn't enough, and seeking professional help becomes necessary. Therapy and counseling can provide invaluable support. Cognitive Behavioral Therapy (CBT) is particularly effective for anxiety disorders, helping you identify and change negative thought patterns. Mindfulness-based therapy is another option, combining traditional therapy with mindfulness practices to help you stay grounded in the present. Finding a qualified mental health professional is key to effective treatment. Look for licensed therapists or counselors with experience in treating anxiety. Online directories and recommendations from friends or healthcare providers can help you find the right fit.

Anxiety is a pervasive issue that many young adults face, but it doesn't have to control your life. By identifying your triggers, employing cognitive behavioral techniques, and using quick relief strategies like breathing exercises, you can manage your anxiety more effectively. Again, seek professional help if necessary. You're taking proactive steps to take care of your mental health, and that's something to be proud of.

Building Resilience: How to Bounce Back from Setbacks

Life is full of setbacks. It's not about avoiding them but learning how to bounce back. That's where resilience comes in. Resilience is your ability to adapt and recover from difficulties. Think of it as your mental and emotional rubber band. Resiliency helps you snap back into shape when stretched by life's challenges. The components of resilience include emotional regulation, optimism, and the ability to see setbacks as temporary. Consider Malala Yousafzai, who turned a traumatic experience into a powerful movement for girls' education. She didn't just survive her setbacks—she used them as stepping stones to achieve greater things.

So, how can you build resilience? Start by developing a growth mindset. This means viewing challenges not as insurmountable obstacles but as opportunities for growth. Carol Dweck's research on growth mindset shows that people who believe their abilities can be developed through effort and learning are more likely to thrive in the face of adversity. Next, focus on building strong social connections. Surround yourself with supportive friends and family who can offer encouragement and perspective. Social support is vital for resilience, providing a sense of belonging and reducing feelings of isolation. Practicing self-compassion also plays a significant role. Be kind to yourself, especially when things go wrong. Instead of berating yourself for mistakes, show yourself the same kindness and compassion you would give a friend. Self-compassion helps you maintain a positive self-image and reduces negative self-talk.

When adversity strikes, it's essential to have practical methods for coping. Reframing negative thoughts is a powerful technique. Instead of thinking, "I failed," reframe it as "I learned what doesn't work." This shift in perspective can reduce the emotional impact of setbacks and help you focus on solutions rather than problems. Setting achievable goals and taking small steps toward them can also make a significant difference.

Break down your larger goals into manageable tasks, and celebrate small victories along the way. This approach makes goals more achievable and builds momentum and confidence. Learning from failures and setbacks is another crucial aspect. View them as valuable lessons that provide insights for future success. Reflect on what went wrong, what you could have done differently, and how to improve moving forward.

Maintaining resilience over time requires ongoing effort and commitment. Regular self-reflection and assessment are essential. Take time to evaluate your progress, identify areas for improvement, and adjust your strategies as needed. Personal development should be a continuous process. Whether it's learning new skills, pursuing hobbies, or seeking new experiences, personal growth keeps you engaged and motivated. Staying connected with a support network is also vital. Regularly check in with friends and family; don't hesitate to seek support when needed. A strong support network can provide encouragement, advice, and a sense of community, all of which are important for long-term resilience.

Building resilience is about developing a mindset and skills that allow you to navigate life's challenges with confidence and grace. Focusing on growth, building strong connections, and practicing self-compassion can enhance your resilience and bounce back from setbacks more effectively. Remember, resilience is not about avoiding difficulties but about facing them head-on and emerging stronger on the other side.

With resilience as your anchor, you're better equipped to tackle life's ups and downs. As we move forward, we'll explore how to create and maintain thriving relationships, another cornerstone of a balanced and fulfilling life.

Key takeaways:

1. Cultivating a practice of daily mindfulness can enhance your mental health by fostering a sense of calm and presence.

2. Learning to manage stress and overcome anxiety through various coping mechanisms can build emotional fortitude.

3. Remember, it's okay to seek professional help when needed. Doing so is a sign of strength, not weakness.

4. Building resilience is finding healthy ways to navigate challenges, ensuring you bounce back stronger.

Chapter 5

Building Strong Relationships

P icture this: you're at a party, trying to strike up a conversation with someone new. You're balancing your drink, trying to remember their name, and hoping you don't say something awkward. Sound familiar? You don't have to be a social butterfly or a mind reader to forge meaningful connections. This chapter is all about helping you master the art of communication, starting with the fundamentals: active listening and empathy.

Effective Communication: Active Listening and Empathy

Ever had a conversation where you felt truly heard? It's like a breath of fresh air, right? Effective communication can transform relationships, making them stronger and more fulfilling. Studies show that good communication skills significantly impact relationship satisfaction. According to *Verywell Mind*, effective communication allows you to share, learn, and respond, forging lasting bonds with others. It's the glue that holds relationships together, whether they're romantic, familial, or friendships.

Active listening is a fundamental part of successful communication. It's not just about hearing words but understanding their meaning and intent. To practice active listening, start by maintaining eye contact. This shows you're engaged and interested in what the other person is saying. Offer verbal and non-verbal feedback, like nodding or saying "I see" to show you're following along. Avoid interrupting the speaker, even if you're bursting with a response. Let them finish their thoughts before you chime in.

Reflecting and paraphrasing what was said can also strengthen your listening skills. For instance, if your friend says, "I'm really stressed about my job," you might respond, "It sounds like work has been overwhelming for you lately." This shows you're paying attention and that you've understood correctly. Active listening helps people feel more understood, building trust and emotional connections.

Building empathy in conversations takes your communication to the next level. Empathy is the ability to understand and share the feelings of another person. Developing empathy can be significantly enhanced by the practice of perspective-taking. This involves making a conscious effort to see situations from the other person's viewpoint, enriching your understanding and connection. Ask yourself how you would feel if you were in their shoes. Recognizing and validating emotions is also vital. If your friend is upset, acknowledge their feelings by saying, "I can see that you're really hurt by this," instead of dismissing their emotions.

Asking open-ended questions can further deepen your understanding and connection. Instead of yes/no questions, try ones that invite more elaborate responses. For example, "How did it feel when that happened?" or "Can you tell me more about that?" These questions encourage the speaker to share more and show that you're genuinely interested in their perspective.

Effective communication isn't without its challenges. Managing distractions during conversations is essential. Put away your phone, close your laptop, and give the speaker your full attention. Addressing language and cultural differences can also be tricky. Be mindful of these differences and ask for clarification if needed. It's better to seek understanding than to make assumptions. Dealing with emotional triggers requires patience and self-awareness. If a topic makes you feel defensive or upset, take a deep breath and remind yourself to stay calm.

Improving communication skills can significantly enhance your relationships. You can forge stronger, more meaningful connections by practicing active listening, building empathy, and overcoming common communication barriers. Remember, communication is a two-way street. It's not just about expressing yourself but also about understanding and responding to others. So, next time you're at that party, balancing your drink and making small talk, remember these tips. They might help you turn an awkward conversation into the start of a beautiful friendship.

Reflection Exercise: Enhancing Communication Skills

1. **Think of a recent conversation**: Reflect on a conversation you had recently. How well did you listen? Did you maintain eye contact and offer feedback?

2. **Practice active listening**: Choose a friend or family member to practice active listening with. Focus on maintaining eye contact, offering feedback, and paraphrasing what they say.

3. **Build empathy**: Next time someone shares their feelings, practice perspective-taking. Try to see the situation from their point of view and acknowledge their emotions.

4. **Overcome barriers**: Identify any common communication barriers you face. Make a plan to manage distractions and address any cultural or language differences in future conversations.

By actively engaging in these exercises, you can enhance your communication skills and build stronger, more empathetic connections.

Conflict Resolution: Handling Disagreements Gracefully

Conflict. Just saying the word might make you uncomfortable. No one likes conflict, but disagreements are totally normal in any healthy relationship. Whether it's a spat with a friend over who flaked on brunch or a more serious argument with a partner about future plans, how you handle these conflicts can make or break the relationship. Effective conflict resolution is fundamental for maintaining healthy relationships. That way disagreements don't fester into resentment and both parties feel heard and respected.

Consider the tale of Jake and Mia. They were roommates who constantly bickered about household chores. Instead of addressing the issue head-on, they let their frustrations build up, leading to a volcanic eruption of arguments. Eventually, they decided to sit down and discuss the issue. By identifying the root cause—different expectations about cleanliness—they were able to find common ground and create a chore schedule. This resolution strengthened their relationship, proving that addressing conflicts directly can lead to positive outcomes. On the flip side, unresolved conflicts can cause significant damage. They can lead to ongoing resentment, lack of trust, and eventually, the breakdown of the relationship. Ignoring issues doesn't make them go away; it just buries them until they resurface with even more intensity.

So, how do you resolve conflicts constructively? Start by identifying the root cause of the conflict. Often, what you're arguing about on the surface isn't the real issue. Maybe the argument about chores is actually about feeling unappreciated. Dig deep to understand the underlying issue. Next, use "I" statements to express your feelings. Instead of saying, "You never help with the chores," try, "I feel overwhelmed when the chores pile up." This approach reduces defensiveness and opens up a more constructive dialogue. Finding common ground and mutual interests is another critical step. Focus on what you both want to achieve, whether it's a cleaner home or more quality time together. Once you've identified mutual goals, brainstorm solutions together. This collaboration helps both parties feel invested in the resolution and are more likely to stick to the agreed-upon plan.

Managing emotions during conflicts is essential for keeping the discussion productive. Deep breathing exercises can help you stay calm. If you feel your temper rising, take a few slow, deep breaths to center yourself. Sometimes, taking a break is necessary. If the conversation becomes too heated, take a short break and revisit the issue when you've both had time to cool down. Practicing mindfulness and self-awareness can also help. Being mindful of your emotions and reactions allows you to respond thoughtfully instead of reacting impulsively.

Handling conflicts in group settings adds another layer of complexity. Whether it's a group project in school or a team meeting at work, conflicts can arise when multiple parties are involved. Start by setting ground rules for discussions. Everyone should agree to listen respectfully and avoid interrupting. Encourage equal participation by giving everyone a chance to voice their opinions. Summarize key points and agreements so that everyone is on the same page. This approach fosters a collaborative environment where all parties feel heard and valued.

Conflict Resolution Exercise: Finding Common Ground

1. **Identify a recent conflict**: Think of a recent disagreement you had with someone. What was the root cause?

2. **Use "I" statements**: Practice expressing your feelings using "I" statements. Write down how you would communicate your feelings without blaming the other person.

3. **Find common ground**: What mutual interests or goals can you identify? How can these help in resolving the conflict?

4. **Brainstorm solutions**: List potential solutions that address both your needs and the other person's. How can you collaborate to implement these solutions?

You can improve your conflict resolution skills and handle disagreements more effectively by actively engaging in this exercise. Remember, conflicts aren't a sign of a bad relationship; they're an opportunity for growth and understanding. Using these techniques, you can navigate conflicts with empathy and patience, leading to stronger, healthier relationships.

Building a Support Network: Finding Your Squad

Imagine trying to navigate life without a reliable support network. It's like trying to build a house without a foundation—doomed to crumble at the first sign of trouble. Having a strong support network is important for emotional wellbeing and personal growth. Social support plays a vital role in mental health, providing a safety net during tough times and a cheering squad during good ones. Studies have shown that people with strong social connections tend to have better mental health, longer lives, and higher levels of wellbeing.

Finding and building relationships might sound difficult sometimes, but it's more accessible than you think. Start by joining clubs or groups that align with your interests. Whether it's a sports team, a hobby group, or a professional association, these settings offer a natural way to meet like-minded people. Volunteering for causes you care about is another excellent strategy. Not only do you contribute to something meaningful, but you also meet others who share your passions and values. Attending social events and gatherings, even if it's a bit outside your comfort zone, can also open doors to new friendships. Whether it's a networking event, a community festival, or a friend's party, these occasions provide opportunities to connect with others.

Once you've built these connections, nurturing and maintaining them is essential. Regular check-ins and communication keep relationships strong. A quick text or a coffee date can go a long way in showing you care. Showing appreciation and gratitude is also imperative. Simple gestures like thanking a friend for their support or acknowledging their achievements can strengthen your bond. Offering support in return is equally important. Be there for your friends during their tough times, just as they are for you. It's a two-way street that guarantees the relationship remains balanced and mutually beneficial.

Balancing old and new relationships requires a bit of juggling but is entirely doable. Setting aside time for both old and new friends helps maintain existing bonds while fostering new ones. Schedule regular catch-ups with your long-time friends and try to integrate new friends into your social circle. This approach strengthens your support network and enriches your social life with diverse perspectives and experiences. Managing potential conflicts between different friend groups might arise, but open communication can help navigate these situations. Be honest about your intentions to bring different groups together and find common activities that everyone can enjoy.

Reflection Section: Building Your Support Network

1. **Identify Your Interests**: List activities or causes you're passionate about. What clubs or groups align with these interests?

2. **Take the First Step**: Choose one activity or event to attend this month. How can you introduce yourself and start a conversation?

3. **Show Appreciation**: Think of a friend who has been supportive. How can you show your gratitude this week?

4. **Schedule Social Time**: Plan a catch-up with an old friend and an outing with a new friend. How can you balance both relationships?

Building a support network is about more than just making friends; it's about creating a community that supports your wellbeing and personal growth. By actively seeking connections, nurturing relationships, and balancing old and new friendships, you can build a robust support system that enriches your life.

Online Etiquette: Cultivating a Positive Social Media Presence

Let's face it, social media is a permanent fixture in our lives. We scroll through our feeds, double-tap photos, and share memes faster than we can say "Wi-Fi." But have you ever stopped to think about the impact your online behavior has on your personal and professional relationships? Your digital footprint is like your online resume. It can either open doors or slam them shut. Building a positive digital footprint isn't just about looking good; it's about being good. How you interact online can avoid misunderstandings and conflicts. Imagine posting a light-hearted joke only to find out it offended someone. That's the kind of digital drama no one needs. Plus, a well-maintained online presence can enhance professional opportunities. Employers often check social media profiles before making hiring decisions. A positive, respectful online persona can tip the scales in your favor.

When it comes to responsible social media use, think before you post. This might sound like common sense, but in the heat of the moment, it's easy to forget. Ask yourself if your post is respectful and if it could be misunderstood. A harmless tweet could be taken out of context and lead to unnecessary conflict. Respecting others' privacy is also paramount. Just because you're comfortable sharing every detail of your life doesn't mean everyone else is. Avoid tagging people in posts without their permission or sharing private conversations. And steer clear of negative or controversial topics unless you're prepared for a potential backlash. It's not about stifling your voice but about choosing your battles wisely.

Social media's impact on mental health is a double-edged sword. On one hand, it connects us with friends, family, and even celebrities. On the other, it can lead to social media burnout. Recognizing the signs of burnout is vital. If you find yourself feeling anxious, depressed, or overwhelmed after scrolling through your feed, it's time to take a break. Set limits on your social media use. Apps like *Screen Time* for iPhone or *Digital Wellbeing* for Android can help you monitor and reduce your usage. Curating a positive feed is another effective strategy. Unfollow accounts that make you feel bad about yourself, and follow those that inspire and uplift you. Your feed should be a source of joy, not stress.

Professional networking on social media is an art form. Platforms like LinkedIn are gold mines for building professional connections. Start by optimizing your LinkedIn profile. Engage with industry-related content by liking, commenting, and sharing posts. This keeps you updated on industry trends and increases your visibility. Join professional groups and discussions to connect with like-minded individuals. These groups are excellent for networking, sharing knowledge, and finding job opportunities. Participating in thoughtful discussions and offering valuable perspectives can help you establish yourself as a thought leader in your field.

In the age of social media, maintaining a positive online presence is more critical than ever. Your digital footprint can impact your personal and professional relationships, so using social media responsibly is a must. You can build a respectful and positive online persona by thinking before you post, respecting others' privacy, and avoiding negative topics. Recognizing the impact of social media on your mental health and taking steps to manage it can help you maintain a healthy relationship with your online world. And by leveraging social media for professional networking, you can open doors to new opportunities and connections. So, scroll wisely and let your online presence reflect the best version of you.

Maintaining Healthy Boundaries: Balancing Personal and Social Life

Ever felt like you're being pulled in a million directions at once? That's what happens when you don't set healthy boundaries. Boundaries are significant for maintaining balance and wellbeing. They help prevent burnout by ensuring you don't overcommit yourself. Imagine trying to be everything to everyone all the time; it's a one-way ticket to exhaustion. Protecting personal time and space is essential for recharging and maintaining your mental health. When you set boundaries, you also enhance the quality of your relationships. People know what to expect from you and respect your limits, which leads to more genuine and fulfilling interactions.

Setting and communicating boundaries might feel awkward at first, but it's a skill worth mastering. Start by identifying your personal limits. What are your non-negotiables? Maybe it's having one weekend day free or not answering work emails after 7 PM. Once you've identified these, communicate them clearly and respectfully. You might say, "I need Sundays to recharge, so I won't be available for meetups." Consistency is key. If you set a boundary, stick to it. This shows others that you take your limits seriously and expect them to do the same.

Respecting others' boundaries is just as important. Always ask for and respect consent. If a friend says they're not up for a late-night chat, don't push it. Being mindful of non-verbal cues can also help. If someone looks uncomfortable or stressed, give them space. And if you cross a boundary, apologize and adjust your behavior. Saying, "I'm sorry, I didn't realize that was a boundary for you. I'll be more mindful next time," goes a long way in maintaining trust and respect.

Common challenges in maintaining boundaries can make the process tricky. Boundary pushers are those who constantly test your limits. They might not respect your need for downtime or try to guilt you into doing things. Stand firm and reiterate your boundaries calmly but assertively. Dealing with guilt and fear of rejection is another hurdle. It's natural to worry that setting boundaries will upset others, but remember that your wellbeing is what matters most. Adjusting boundaries as needed is a part of the process. Life changes, and so might your limits. Be flexible and willing to reassess your boundaries as circumstances shift.

Balancing your social life with personal time is an ongoing act. Scheduling downtime and self-care activities is necessary. Block out time in your calendar for activities that recharge you, whether it's reading, hiking, or just binge-watching your favorite show. Saying no to social invitations without guilt is a powerful skill. Politely declining an invite with, "I need some time to myself this weekend, but let's catch up soon," is perfectly okay. Finding a healthy balance between socializing and alone time helps you not neglect your own needs. It's about quality over quantity. Spend time with people who uplift and energize you, and don't feel obligated to attend every event.

Boundaries are not about building walls but about setting guidelines that protect your wellbeing and strengthen your relationships. They help you maintain balance, prevent burnout, and make sure that your interactions with others are respectful and fulfilling. By identifying your limits, communicating them clearly, and respecting the boundaries of others, you create a healthier, more balanced life. Balancing social commitments with personal time is an ongoing process, but with practice, it becomes second nature.

Maintaining healthy boundaries is about creating a life where you feel in control and respected. As we wrap up this chapter, remember that boundaries are your personal rules for how you want to be treated. They're essential for your mental health and the quality of your relationships. Next, we'll explore how to navigate the transition to living independently, a pivotal step in adulting that brings its own set of challenges and rewards.

Key takeaways:

1. Effective communication is the foundation of any healthy relationship.

2. Learn to express your needs and listen actively.

3. Conflict resolution skills are crucial for navigating disagreements constructively.

4. Cultivating a support network of friends, family, and mentors can provide a solid foundation during challenging times.

5. Setting and respecting healthy boundaries is vital for maintaining personal wellbeing and relationship health.

Make a Difference with Your Review

Unlock the Power of Generosity

"The best way to find yourself is to lose yourself in the service of others." – Mahatma Gandhi

Adulting is tough. That's why this book exists—to make the transition to adulthood a little easier, a little less scary, and a whole lot more doable. But here's the thing: we can't reach every young adult out there without your help.

Would you lend a hand to someone just like you? Someone who's curious about adulting life skills but unsure where to begin?

Why Your Review Matters

The truth is, most people decide what to read based on reviews. Your voice can make a real difference in helping others take the first step toward mastering adulting life skills. By sharing your thoughts, you can:

- Encourage one more young adult to feel confident navigating life's challenges.

- Help one more person crush their goals and dreams.

- Show one more reader that adulting isn't just about surviving—it's about thriving.

It costs nothing, takes just a minute, and could be the nudge someone needs to start their journey.

How to Leave a Review

Making a difference is simple:

1. Scan the QR code below or click this link: https://www.amazon .com/review/review-your-purchases/?asin=B0DWX3SBX6

2. Write a quick review—just a few sentences about what you found helpful or what made you smile.

If you believe in helping others, you're exactly the kind of person who makes the world brighter. Thank you for being a part of this mission!

With gratitude,
IRL Publishing
In. Real. Life.

Chapter 6

Moving Out On Your Own

S o you've finally got the keys to your first place. You're standing at the threshold, feeling a mix of excitement and terror. The world is your oyster, but you're now responsible for everything from paying rent to fixing that weird noise the fridge makes. Moving out on your own is a monumental step, a rite of passage that screams independence. But before you start packing your bags and booking a U-Haul, there's a lot to consider. Let's start with the basics: finding the right place to live.

Housing: Finding the Right Place to Live

The first big decision is whether to rent or buy. Renting is usually the go-to option for young adults, especially if you're not ready to commit to one location for the long haul. Renting offers flexibility and lower upfront costs. You pay a security deposit and monthly rent and are good to go. Plus, if the toilet breaks, it's your landlord's problem, not yours. Buying, on the other hand, is more complicated. It involves a hefty down payment, a mortgage, and maintenance responsibilities. But it is an investment. Over time, you build equity, and one day, you might be able to sell your place for a profit. If you're considering buying, make sure you're financially stable and ready to settle down for at least a few years.

Let's talk about types of housing. Apartments are a popular choice when starting out. They're usually more affordable and have amenities like gyms, pools, and laundry facilities. Plus, you're not responsible for maintenance. Shared housing, like renting a room in a house with roommates, can be a budget-friendly option too. It's pretty common in cities with high living costs. You split rent and utilities, saving you a lot of money. Single-family homes are another option, but they tend to be more expensive and have more responsibilities. If you love the idea of a backyard and more privacy, this could be your dream setup. Just be prepared for the extra work and cost.

Now, let's dive into location considerations. Being close to work, school, and amenities is a real convenience. You don't want to spend half your life commuting, if you can help it. Look for places that are close to restaurants, grocery stores, and other necessities. Living nearby can save you time and stress if you're in college or have a job downtown. Neighborhood safety is another big factor. Research crime rates to get a feel for the area. You can use websites like *NeighborhoodScout* or local police department resources to check crime statistics. A safe neighborhood gives you peace of mind and protects your property and wellbeing.

You might not think about the community vibe initially, but it's super important. Do you want a bustling area with many young professionals and nightlife, or do you prefer a quieter, family-oriented neighborhood? Visit the area at different times of the day to get a sense of the community. Check out local events, parks, and eateries. The right community can make your new place feel like home.

Choosing where to live is a big decision, and it's not just about finding a place with decent rent. It's about finding a space that fits your lifestyle and meets your needs. Whether you rent a cozy apartment, share a house with friends, or invest in a single-family home, consider all the factors. Your new place should be a sanctuary where you feel safe, comfortable, and happy.

And remember, no matter where you end up, you can always make it feel like home with a little effort and creativity.

Need a Roommate? Tips to Choose the Right One

Thinking about getting a roommate? It's like dating but without the romantic dinners and awkward first kisses. Still, having a roommate can be a game-changer. For starters, sharing rent and utilities can save you a ton of money. Imagine cutting your rent in half—that's more cash for fun stuff like concert tickets, new clothes, or that new restaurant everyone keeps talking about. Plus, having someone to share the responsibilities of maintaining a home can take a lot of the pressure off. No more solo dishwashing marathons or tackling the bathroom grime alone. Sharing chores mean more free time and less stress.

However, not all roommates are created equal, so evaluating potential ones is super important. Think about lifestyle and habits. Are you a night owl who loves blasting music at 2 a.m., while your potential roommate is an early bird who cherishes their morning yoga routine? That could be trouble. Lifestyle compatibility can make or break your living situation. Then, there's communication style and conflict resolution. If one of you is a "talk it out" type and the other is more of a "silent treatment" kind of person, things can escalate quickly. Look for someone who communicates openly and resolves issues calmly. Financial reliability is another biggie. You don't want to cover their share of the rent because they blew it all on a weekend trip. Make sure they have a steady income and fully understand shared financial responsibilities.

Finding the right roommate might seem challenging, but there are plenty of resources to help you. *Facebook* has groups dedicated to housing and roommates. Roommate-matching services like *Roomster* or *Common* can also connect you with potential housemates. Community boards at local coffee shops or online forums like Reddit can be gold mines for roommate searches. Once you've found a few candidates, it's time to conduct interviews. Yes, interviews. Ask questions about their daily routines, cleaning habits, and how they handle conflicts. It might feel a bit formal, but it's better to know upfront if you're dealing with a neat freak or someone who thinks dishes should soak for a week.

Setting expectations with a roommate is like setting the rules for a game—to make sure everyone knows how to play. Start by establishing house rules. Who takes out the trash? What's the policy on overnight guests? Having clear guidelines can prevent misunderstandings and keep the peace. Discuss privacy and personal space boundaries too. Maybe you're cool with sharing snacks, but not your favorite hoodie. Make sure you both understand and respect each other's boundaries. Creating a roommate agreement might sound over the top, but it can save a lot of headaches. Outline the rules, responsibilities, and what happens if someone decides to move out early. It doesn't have to be a formal document, but having everything in writing can prevent future disagreements.

Living with a roommate can be an amazing experience if you choose the right person and set clear expectations. It's all about finding someone compatible, communicating openly, and sharing responsibilities fairly. So, take your time, ask the right questions, and set the ground rules. Your future self will thank you.

Signing a Lease: What to Look For and What to Avoid

You've found the perfect place and are ready to sign the lease. Hold up! Before you put pen to paper, make sure you understanding the lease terms. Reading and comprehending your lease can save you from unexpected costs and obligations. Consider it the fine print in a contract—ignore it, and you might find yourself paying for your neighbor's cat's medical bills.

Protecting your rights as a tenant guarantees you get fair terms. A lease agreement is a legally binding document outlining your rental's dos and don'ts. Missing the small details can lead to big headaches. For example, there might be hidden fees in the agreement that weren't mentioned. You might think you're paying $1,200 a month, but add in "administrative fees" and "maintenance costs," suddenly, you're shelling out $1,500. Then, there are restrictive clauses. Imagine signing a lease only to find out you can't have overnight guests or need the landlord's permission to hang a picture on the wall. These issues are more common than you'd think.

Now, let's break down the key components of a lease agreement. First up is the rent amount and payment terms. This section should clearly state how much you owe each month, when it's due, and what forms of payment are accepted. Some landlords prefer checks, while others are okay with electronic transfers. Next, look at the duration of the lease and renewal options. Most leases are for a year, but some might be longer or even month-to-month. Renewal clauses are also important; they outline what happens at the end of the lease term. Do you automatically renew, or do you need to give notice?

Security deposit details are another important element. Your lease should specify how much you must pay upfront and under what conditions you'll get it back. Typically, security deposits cover potential property damage, but these days, they can also cover cleaning from normal wear after you move out. Make sure this section is clear to avoid any disputes when you move out. Maintenance and repair responsibilities should also be outlined. Who's responsible for fixing a leaky faucet or a broken window? Knowing this upfront can save you from unexpected repair bills.

Keep an eye out for common red flags in lease agreements. Excessive penalties for breaking the lease are a major one. Life happens, and sometimes you need to move out early. Make sure you understand what the penalties are and if they're reasonable. Ambiguous language or missing details can also be problematic. If something isn't clear, ask for clarification. Restrictions on guests or subletting can be a dealbreaker. Some leases have strict rules about who can stay over and how often, or whether you can sublet your place if you need to. Unreasonable rules or requirements can make your life miserable. If the lease is filled with restrictions, it might be worth looking elsewhere.

Before signing the lease, take some necessary steps. Inspect the property for any issues. Don't just glance around; open cabinets, check for leaks, and be sure that everything works. This step is to establish the condition of the property before you move in so that you are not liable for any identified issues when you move out. Clarify any unclear terms with the landlord. If something doesn't make sense, ask questions until it does. Finally, keep a copy of the signed lease for reference. You never know when you might need to reference it.

Understanding lease agreements might not be the most exciting part of moving out, but it's one of the most important. By being thorough and cautious, you can avoid unnecessary stress and enjoy a smooth renting experience.

It's Moving Day! Getting Prepared For the Big Day

Moving day is like gearing up for a marathon, but instead of running shoes, you need boxes, tape, and a solid plan. Choosing a moving date is your first hurdle. Aim for a weekday if possible; weekends are peak times and can be more expensive. Once you've locked in a date, decide whether to hire movers or do it yourself. Professional movers can save you a lot of stress, but they come with a price tag. If you're on a budget, rally some friends and rent a truck. Just remember to thank them with pizza and drinks.

The way you pack can make a world of difference. Start early and pack room by room. Label each box clearly with its contents and the room it belongs in, like kitchen, bedroom, bathroom. Use smaller boxes for heavy items like books and larger ones for lighter, bulkier items like bedding. Wrap fragile items in bubble wrap or towels to keep them safe. Keep a separate box of the things you'll need the first night—think bathroom stuff, a change of clothes, and basic kitchen supplies. This way, you won't be digging through boxes at midnight just to find your toothbrush.

Notifying important parties about your move is the next step. Change your address with the post office so that your mail follows you to your new place. It's a simple process you can do online at www.usps.com. Inform your bank, credit card companies, and any subscription services you use. The last thing you want is for important documents to end up at your old address. Not a huge deal if you're moving from your parent's house nearby, but good to take care of anyway. Don't forget to update your address with your employer and any institutions you're affiliated with, like your school or gym. This helps you stay in the loop and not miss out on any communications.

Setting up utilities ahead of time is a step you do not want to miss. Imagine moving into your new place only to find out you have no electricity or internet—nightmare scenario, right? Contact utility companies at least two weeks before your move to schedule the transfer of services. This includes electricity, gas, internet, and any other services you need. For electricity and gas, you'll usually need to provide your new address and the date you want the service to start. For internet, research providers in your area and choose a plan that fits your needs. Some providers may have installation fees, so budget for that as well.

Understanding your utility bills can help you reduce costs. Electricity is often the biggest expense. Be mindful of your usage. Turn off lights when you leave a room, unplug electronics when not in use, and consider energy-efficient appliances. For water, simple changes like taking shorter showers and fixing leaks right away can make a big difference. Internet costs can add up, too. If you're not a heavy user, opt for a basic plan.

Moving day doesn't have to be crazy. With some planning and some strategic decisions, you can make the transition smooth and stress-free. Choose your moving date wisely, decide between hiring movers or DIY, and pack efficiently. Notify important parties about your move so you don't miss anything. Set up your utilities ahead of time and understand your bills to avoid unnecessary costs. This way, you can focus on what really matters—settling into your new home and starting this exciting chapter of your life.

Sharing Your Home: How to Cohabitate Peacefully

Moving in with someone else can feel like you're stepping into a reality show, complete with unexpected plot twists and drama. But with the right strategies, you can turn your shared living space into a peaceful haven. First up, let's talk about dividing responsibilities. Splitting up the chores and household duties is important when sharing a home. Make a list of all the tasks that need to be done—cleaning, taking out the trash, doing the dishes, etc. Sit down with your roommate or partner and divide these tasks based on preference and schedules. Some people might prefer doing dishes over vacuuming, so play to each other's strengths. Rotating responsibilities can also keep things balanced. This way, no one feels like they're always stuck with the worst tasks. For example, you could switch who cleans the bathroom every week. This maintains balance and keeps tasks from becoming monotonous for either of you.

Handling shared expenses is another area where clear communication is necessary. When it comes to splitting rent, utilities, and other shared costs, transparency is your best friend. You can use apps like *Splitwise* or *Venmo* to keep track of who owes what. These apps allow you to log expenses in real time, ensuring that everyone is on the same page. It might also be helpful to establish a budget for shared expenses to avoid any surprises. This way, you can plan and save for bigger costs together, like a new couch or a shared streaming service.

Conflict resolution is an inevitable part of cohabitation. The goal isn't to avoid conflicts altogether but to address them calmly and effectively when they arise. Open communication is critical here. If something is bothering you, bring it up sooner rather than later. For instance, if your roommate's habit of leaving dirty dishes in the sink drives you crazy, mention it right away rather than letting it fester. Addressing issues calmly and without blame can prevent small annoyances from turning into major conflicts. It's also helpful to approach these conversations with a problem-solving mindset. Instead of pointing fingers, focus on finding a solution that works for everyone.

Respecting shared spaces is one of the best ways to keep the peace with a roommate. Maintaining a clean and organized common area takes effort from both parties. This means not leaving personal items scattered around and cleaning up after yourself. Discuss noise levels and establish quiet hours if needed. For example, if one of you works from home while the other works nights, set specific times when noise should be kept to a minimum. The same goes for guests. Talk about how often you can have people over and how long they can stay. This prevents any awkward situations where one person feels like their home has turned into a social club.

Lastly, respecting each other's use of shared items can go a long way in maintaining harmony. Whether it's the TV remote, kitchen utensils, or even the washing machine, make sure to discuss and agree on how these items will be shared. For example, if one person loves to cook elaborate meals and the other prefers takeout, work out a schedule for kitchen use that makes everyone happy. This guarantees that shared spaces and items are used fairly and that everyone's needs are met.

Living with someone else doesn't have to be a constant battle. By dividing responsibilities, handling shared expenses transparently, resolving conflicts calmly, and respecting shared spaces, you can create a harmonious living situation. Remember, successful cohabitation is all about communication, compromise, and mutual respect.

Tenant Rights: Knowing Your Legal Protections

Knowing your tenant rights is like having a superpower in the adulting world. It provides fair treatment by landlords and protects you from unlawful evictions and discrimination. Imagine moving into your dream apartment, only to find that your landlord decides to kick you out because they don't like your pet. Or worse, they hike up the rent without any notice. Understanding your rights can save you from these nightmares.

Every renter should know their basic rights. First, you have the right to a habitable living environment. This means your landlord is responsible for making sure that your home is safe, clean, and compliant with health codes. Broken heaters, leaky roofs, and pest infestations are not just annoyances but violations. You also have the right to privacy and quiet enjoyment. Your landlord can't barge in whenever they feel like it. They must provide notice before entering your home, usually 24-48 hours. Protection against retaliatory eviction is another right. If you report a problem or file a complaint, your landlord can't evict you out of spite. Procedures for requesting repairs should be clearly outlined in your lease. Your landlord is required to make necessary repairs in a timely manner. Know the process and follow it to make sure your home remains livable.

Handling disputes with landlords can be tricky, but it's manageable with the right approach. Start by documenting issues and communications. Keep a log of problems, take photos, and save all correspondence. This documentation may be necessary if things escalate. When requesting repairs or addressing concerns, send written requests. Emails work, but some communities have an app or website where you can submit maintenance requests online. If your landlord is unresponsive, consider using mediation services. These services can help both parties reach a fair agreement without going to court. However, knowing when to seek legal assistance is vital if the issue remains unresolved and your rights are being violated. Legal aid services can provide guidance and representation if necessary.

Resources for tenant rights information and support are plentiful. Local tenant unions or associations are great places to start. They often provide free advice and can guide you through the maze of tenant laws. Legal aid services are another valuable resource. They offer free or low-cost legal help to tenants facing disputes. Government housing agencies can provide information on your rights and local housing laws. Online resources and guides are also incredibly helpful. Websites like *Nolo* and the *U.S. Department of Housing and Urban Development (HUD)* offer detailed information on tenant rights.

Incorporating these practices into your life will help you confidently navigate the complexities of renting. Understanding your rights ensures you are treated fairly and can enjoy your home without unnecessary stress. By knowing your rights, documenting issues, and seeking help when needed, you can protect yourself from unfair treatment and live more comfortably. Your home should be your sanctuary, and knowing your tenant rights is the first step in making that a reality. As you move forward, keep these protections in mind, and you'll be well-equipped to handle any challenges that come your way.

Key takeaways:

1. When moving out, consider your needs and budget to find the right place.

2. Choosing a compatible roommate can enhance your living experience.

3. Understanding lease agreements and your rights as a tenant can prevent future disputes.

Chapter 7

Cooking and Nutrition Made Easy

E ver opened your fridge and felt like you were staring into a black hole of mismatched leftovers and expired condiments? Cooking can seem overwhelming when your culinary repertoire consists of microwave dinners and instant noodles. But trust me, you can turn your kitchen into a culinary playground with the right tools and techniques. Let's get started with the basics.

Cooking 101: Essential Kitchen Tools and Techniques

Having the proper kitchen tools is like having a superhero team at your disposal. They make cooking more efficient, enjoyable, and safe. Try building a house with a plastic hammer—it won't end well. The same goes for cooking. Good tools can make a world of difference in your meal prep. They save you time, reduce the risk of accidents, and help you achieve better cooking results. So, what are these magical tools, you ask?

- First up, the **chef's knife**. A good chef's knife is necessary for almost everything you do in the kitchen, from chopping vegetables to slicing meat. When starting out, don't worry about having a top-of-the-line knife; even a $20 chef's knife from Target can do wonders. Pair this with a sturdy **cutting board**, preferably hardwood like walnut or bamboo. Avoid glass or plastic boards; they can dull your knives and are less sanitary.

- Next, you need **measuring cups and spoons**. Precision is key in cooking, especially baking. Pyrex measuring cups are great for liquids; they're sturdy and microwave-safe. For dry ingredients, OXO's measuring cups are a solid choice. Long, narrow measuring spoons that fit into spice jars are a lifesaver.

- Don't forget a **large, heavy pot** for boiling pasta or blanching vegetables.

Let's talk techniques now that you're armed with the right tools.

- **Sautéing** is one of the fundamental cooking methods. Heat a little oil in your skillet, and once it's shimmering, add your ingredients. Stir them around until they're cooked through, and you've just sautéed.

- **Boiling** is another basic technique. Fill your large pot with water, bring it to a rolling boil, add a pinch of salt, and then toss in your pasta or veggies.

- **Roasting** is perfect for bringing out the natural flavors of your food. Preheat your oven, toss your ingredients with some oil and seasoning, spread them out on a sheet tray, and let the oven work its magic.

- **Grilling**, whether on a barbecue or a grill pan, adds that delicious charred flavor. Just preheat, oil the grates, and cook your food until it's got those beautiful grill marks.

Safety in the kitchen is non-negotiable. Always handle knives with care. Keep your fingers tucked in, and use a stable cutting board. When using the stovetop, be sure pot handles are turned inward to avoid accidentally knocking into a hot pan. Fire safety is critical—having a fire extinguisher in the kitchen is advised. If a grease fire occurs, never use water to extinguish it; smother it with a lid or use a fire extinguisher.

Setting up your pantry is the next step. Stock it with some basic ingredients like:

- Salt

- Pepper

- Garlic powder

- Olive oil

- Vegetable oil

- Rice

- Pasta

- Canned goods

With these items on hand, you'll be ready to whip up a meal at a moment's notice.

So there you have it—a crash course to get you started. Armed with the right tools and basic techniques, you're well on your way to becoming a kitchen ninja. No more staring into the abyss of your fridge, wondering what to make. Instead, you'll be confidently whipping up delicious meals, impressing friends, and, most importantly, feeding yourself. Now, let's get cooking!

Meal Planning Basics: Creating a Weekly Meal Plan

Meal planning might sound like something only super-organized people do, but trust me, it's a game-changer. Imagine knowing exactly what you're going to eat for the week, having all the ingredients ready, and not scrambling to figure out dinner after a long day. Meal planning can save you time and money and reduce food waste. According to a study, people who plan their meals are more likely to make healthier food choices and save money by avoiding impulse purchases.

Creating a weekly meal plan starts with choosing the right app. There are plenty out there, like *Mealime* or *Plan to Eat*, which can simplify the process. *Mealime* offers personalized meal plans based on dietary preferences and can generate grocery lists. Online recipe databases like *AllRecipes* or *Bon Appetit* provide endless inspiration. You can bookmark your favorite recipes for future use. Start by selecting recipes for the week. Think about your schedule: if you know you'll have a busy Wednesday, plan for something quick and easy, like a sandwich or a salad. Once you have your recipes, create a shopping list based on the ingredients required. This helps you buy only what you need, reducing waste and saving money.

To make meal planning more effective and enjoyable, incorporate variety to avoid meal burnout. No one wants to eat chicken and rice five days in a row. Mix things up with different cuisines and ingredients. Flexibility is important. If you planned for spaghetti on Thursday but suddenly crave tacos, it's okay to swap meals. Involving family or roommates in the planning process can also make it more fun and guarantee that everyone's preferences are considered. Maybe your roommate has a killer recipe for chili, or your partner loves making homemade pizza.

Meal planning may seem like a lot of work upfront, but the benefits are worth it. You'll find yourself less stressed about what to cook, saving money by sticking to a grocery list and reducing food waste by using all the ingredients you buy. Plus, there's something incredibly satisfying about having a plan and knowing you're prepared for the week ahead. So grab your phone, pick an app, and start planning your meals. You'll wonder how you ever managed without it.

Grocery Shopping Tips: Getting the Best Deals

Grocery shopping might not be the glamorous part of adulting, but it's definitely one of the most necessary. Let's talk about cutting your grocery bill without sacrificing quality. It's all about strategy. First up, shopping sales and using coupons can make a huge difference. Keep an eye on weekly ads and make a list of items on sale. Coupons are another goldmine. You can find them in newspapers, online, or through apps like *Honey*. Combine sales and coupons for maximum savings. Another tip is buying in bulk, especially for non-perishable items like rice, pasta, and canned goods. Bulk stores like Costco offer great deals, but make sure you have the storage space. Lastly, don't shy away from store brands. They're often just as good as name brands but much cheaper. A box of store-brand cereal can save you a couple of bucks, which adds up over time.

Creating an efficient grocery shopping list is your next step. An organized list saves you time and keeps you focused, reducing the temptation to buy things you don't need. Start by categorizing items by section of the store—produce, dairy, meat, boxed and canned goods. This way, you can avoid zigzagging across the store, saving time and reducing impulse buys. Some stores like Ralphs/Kroger have an app that allows you to create your shopping list and directs you through the store aisle by aisle. Apps like *AnyList* or *Google Keep* can help you keep track of your list too. They let you add items as you think of them and even share the list with family or roommates. Stick to your list like it's a lifeline. Impulse purchases are budget busters; those snacks and extras can quickly add up.

Understanding food labels and expiration dates can be a bit confusing, but it's helpful for making healthier choices. Food labels provide nutritional information that can help you make informed decisions. For instance, check the serving size first. It's easy to consume more calories than you think when the serving size is smaller than what you're eating. Look out for nutrients you need to limit, like saturated fat, sodium, and added sugars, and focus on those you need more of, like dietary fiber, vitamin D, and calcium. The "sell by" date tells the store how long to display the product, while the "use by" date is the manufacturer's recommendation for peak quality. Understanding these dates helps you avoid unnecessary waste and helps guarantee you're eating food at its best.

If you're looking to help the planet, you can make several simple changes. Bringing reusable bags is a no-brainer. They reduce plastic waste and are sturdier for carrying your groceries. Next, opt for products with minimal packaging. Items like loose fruits and vegetables or bulk bin grains cut down on waste and are often cheaper. Supporting local farmers' markets is another great way to shop sustainably. You get fresh, seasonal produce while supporting local agriculture. Plus, the food often tastes better because it's picked at peak ripeness.

Avoiding common grocery shopping pitfalls can save you time, money, and frustration. One of the biggest mistakes is shopping while hungry. When you're hungry, everything looks delicious, and you're more likely to make impulse purchases. Eat a snack before you go to avoid this trap. Also, be careful of overbuying perishable items. It's easy to get carried away in the produce aisle, but you're just wasting money if you buy more than you can eat before it goes bad. Plan your meals and buy only what you need, so everything gets used.

Grocery shopping doesn't have to be a dreaded chore. With a few smart strategies, you can save money, eat better, and even enjoy the process. So next time you head to the store, armed with your list and a full stomach, you'll be ready to conquer those aisles like a pro.

Easy and Healthy Recipes: From Breakfast to Dinner

Balanced, healthy meals are like the fuel for your life's engine. They keep you running smoothly, give you energy, and help you tackle whatever the day throws at you. A balanced diet is essential because it incorporates various nutrients your body needs to function at its best. Foods like leafy greens, whole grains, lean proteins, and colorful fruits and vegetables pack a punch in terms of vitamins, minerals, and antioxidants. They help maintain overall health, boosting your immune system and keeping your energy levels steady throughout the day.

Let's kick off with **breakfast**, often touted as the most important meal of the day. And no, a cup of coffee doesn't count! Starting your day with a nutritious breakfast sets the tone for healthy eating habits.

- Overnight oats are a lifesaver. Mix rolled oats and your choice of milk with a dollop of Greek yogurt, and refrigerate overnight. In the morning, add fruits, nuts, or a drizzle of honey.

- Smoothie bowls are another quick, healthy option. Blend your favorite fruits with some Greek yogurt or a splash of almond milk, pour it into a bowl, and add granola, chia seeds, and fresh berries.

- If you prefer something warm, a veggie-packed omelet is your go-to. Beat a couple of eggs, pour them into a hot pan, and add chopped vegetables like bell peppers, spinach, and tomatoes. Sprinkle a little cheese if you like, and you've got a protein-rich, satisfying breakfast.

When **lunchtime** rolls around, you want something quick and nutritious that you can take on the go.

- Mason jar salads are not only Instagram-worthy but also incredibly practical. Layer your favorite salad ingredients in a mason jar, starting with the dressing at the bottom, followed by hearty ingredients like beans or grains, and finishing with leafy greens on top. Shake it up when you're ready to eat.

- Whole-grain wraps are another easy option. Grab a whole grain tortilla, spread some hummus or avocado, add lean protein like grilled chicken or turkey, and pile on the veggies. Roll it up, and you're good to go.

- Quinoa bowls with roasted vegetables are both filling and nutritious. Cook some quinoa, roast a variety of vegetables like sweet potatoes, broccoli, and carrots, and toss them together with a simple dressing of olive oil and lemon juice.

Dinner can be tricky, especially after a long day when the last thing you want to do is spend hours in the kitchen. But who says healthy dinners need to be time-consuming?

- One-pan roasted chicken and veggies are a breeze. Toss chicken breasts and your favorite vegetables (think cauliflower, zucchini, and cherry tomatoes) with olive oil and your favorite seasonings, spread them out on a baking sheet, and roast until everything is cooked through.

- Stir-fry is another quick and versatile option. Sauté assorted vegetables like mushrooms, snap peas, and carrots with tofu or your choice of protein in a hot pan with a splash of soy sauce and a sprinkle of sesame seeds. Serve it over brown rice or noodles, and dinner is ready in no time.

- Feeling like pasta but want to keep it light? Spaghetti squash with marinara sauce is your answer. Cut a spaghetti squash in half, scoop out the seeds, and roast it until tender. Use a fork to shred the squash into spaghetti-like strands and top it with your favorite marinara sauce and a little Parmesan cheese.

Balanced, healthy meals don't have to be complicated or time-consuming. With these simple recipes, you can start your day with a nutritious breakfast, enjoy a quick and easy lunch, and whip up a healthy dinner even on your busiest evenings. So, grab your apron and get cooking.

Quick and Healthy Snacks: Fueling Your Body on the Go

Snacking gets a bad rap, but when done right, it can be your best ally. Nutritious snacks keep your energy levels steady and prevent overeating at meal times. Think of snacks as mini fuel-ups that keep your engine running smoothly throughout the day. Regular, balanced snacks can relieve that dreaded afternoon slump and help you stay focused. Avoiding high-sugar and high-fat options is key. Instead, go for snacks rich in protein, fiber, and healthy fats. These nutrients keep you feeling full and satisfied longer, reducing the temptation for unhealthy binges.

Let's talk about some quick and healthy snack recipes.

- Homemade granola bars are a great option. Mix rolled oats, honey, almond butter, nuts, and dried fruits. Press the mixture into a baking dish, chill, and cut into bars. These are perfect for grabbing on the way out the door.

- Veggie sticks with hummus are another easy, nutritious snack. Chop up carrots, cucumbers, and bell peppers, and pair them with hummus for a crunchy, satisfying treat.

- Greek yogurt with fruit and nuts is also a winner. Grab a cup of Greek yogurt, add some fresh berries, and sprinkle with a mix of nuts and seeds. It's a snack that's both creamy and crunchy, hitting all the right notes.

Prepping snacks in advance can make healthy eating a breeze. Portioning your snacks into containers at the beginning of the week saves time so that you have healthy options ready to go. Use small containers or reusable snack bags to store your snacks. Keep perishable items like yogurt and veggie sticks in the fridge, while granola bars and nuts can be stored in the pantry. Having these prepped and ready means you don't have to reach for a bag of chips when hunger strikes.

Sometimes, life gets busy, and you might not have time to prep snacks. That's where store-bought options come in handy. Nut butters and whole grain crackers provide a good balance of protein and carbs. Look for options with minimal ingredients to avoid added sugars and unhealthy fats. Pre-cut fruit and veggie packs are also a great choice. They're convenient and fresh and save you the hassle of chopping. Low-sugar protein bars can be lifesavers on particularly hectic days. Just be sure to check the labels and choose bars with natural ingredients and low added sugars.

So, there you have it. Snacking doesn't have to be your nemesis. With a bit of planning and some smart choices, you can keep your body fueled and your energy levels stable. Whether you're at home, at work, or on the go, having nutritious snacks on hand can make a world of difference in maintaining a balanced diet and a healthy lifestyle.

Key takeaways:

1. Equipping your kitchen with essential tools and learning to plan meals can make cooking at home a breeze.

2. Smart grocery shopping and meal prep can save you money and support a healthy diet.

3. Exploring simple, healthy recipes can be a fun and rewarding way to take charge of your nutrition.

Chapter 8
Household Management Skills

Remember when you couldn't find your favorite pair of socks because your room looked like a tornado hit it? Or when you decided to clean your bathroom for the first time in weeks and discovered you might have inadvertently created a new species of mold? Yeah, we've all been there. Welcome to the world of household management, where keeping your living space clean and organized is not just about impressing your mom when she visits, but actually creating a healthier and more comfortable environment for yourself. Let's dive into why a cleaning routine is your new best friend and how you can master it.

Cleaning Tips: Daily, Weekly, and Monthly Checklists

Maintaining a regular cleaning schedule is vital for a healthy and comfortable living environment. It's not just about avoiding the embarrassment of unexpected guests; it's about creating a space where you can relax and be productive. Regular cleaning helps reduce allergens and germs, which can seriously affect your health. Dust, pet dander, and mold are common allergens that love to settle in untouched corners. A clean home minimizes these and keeps you breathing easy. Additionally, keeping clutter at bay prevents the overwhelming feeling that can come from seeing piles of stuff everywhere. A tidy space can increase productivity by providing a calm and focused environment. When your surroundings are in order, your mind can be too.

Starting with daily cleaning tasks, these are the small but mighty chores that keep your home from descending into chaos. First up, making your bed. It might seem trivial, but this simple act sets a productive tone for the day. Plus, climbing into a neatly made bed at night is a small luxury that's totally worth it. Next, wipe down kitchen counters and sinks. This prevents the buildup of food particles and bacteria, keeping your kitchen hygienic. After preparing meals, a quick wipe with a disinfectant can go a long way. Lastly, put away clutter. Designate a spot for everything and make it a habit to return items to their place. This keeps your space organized and saves you time searching for things.

Weekly cleaning tasks are the backbone of maintaining a clean home. Vacuuming and mopping floors come first. Vacuuming removes dust and dirt from carpets and floors while mopping disinfects and leaves your floors sparkling. High-traffic areas might need more frequent attention, but once a week is a good rule of thumb. Cleaning bathrooms is next on the list. This means scrubbing toilets, sinks, and showers. Use a good bathroom cleaner to tackle soap scum and mildew. Regular cleaning prevents the buildup of grime and keeps your bathroom fresh. Don't forget to dust surfaces and fixtures. Dusting removes allergens and keeps your home looking neat. Pay special attention to areas like shelves, light fixtures, and ceiling fans.

TIP: Avoid using bleach cleaning products if your bath/shower is fiberglass, not porcelain or tile. Bleach will degrade the surface and cause permanent stains to set in. Some apartment lease contracts will also specify this.

Monthly deep cleaning tasks are the heavy hitters. These chores don't need daily or weekly attention but will contribute to a thoroughly clean home. Start with cleaning windows and mirrors. Crystal-clear windows let in more light, brightening your space and your mood. Use a streak-free cleaner and a microfiber cloth for the best results. Next, wipe down baseboards and vents. These often-overlooked areas will accumulate dust and grime. A quick wipe with a damp cloth keeps them clean and prevents the buildup of allergens. Finally, declutter and organize storage spaces. Go through closets, cabinets, and drawers to get rid of items you no longer need. Organizing these spaces makes it easier to find what you're looking for and keeps your home tidy.

Daily, Weekly, and Monthly Cleaning Checklist

Daily Tasks:
- Make the bed

- Wipe down kitchen counters and sinks

- Put away clutter

Weekly Tasks:
- Vacuum and mop floors

- Clean bathrooms (toilets, sinks, showers)

- Dust surfaces and fixtures

Monthly Tasks:
- Clean windows and mirrors

- Wipe down baseboards and vents

- Declutter and organize storage spaces

Keeping a clean home doesn't have to be overwhelming. You can maintain a tidy and healthy living environment with minimal effort by breaking it down into daily, weekly, and monthly tasks. Plus, you'll always be ready for those surprise visits from friends or family. Happy cleaning!

Laundry 101: From Sorting to Folding

So you're digging through a pile of laundry, and you find your once-white shirt now a sad shade of pink. Laundry disasters happen, but they don't have to. Sorting laundry effectively can prevent these mishaps and make sure your clothes come out clean and fresh. Start by separating your laundry by color. Whites, darks, and colors should each get their own pile. Whites stay bright when washed together, while darks won't bleed onto lighter fabrics. Colors, especially bright ones, need their own space to avoid dye transfer. If you don't have enough whites to justify a separate load, you can simply sort lights and darks. Always washing in cold water can help minimize the chances that colors will run.

Next, consider the fabric type. Heavy fabrics like jeans and towels need more intense wash cycles, whereas delicates like silk and lace require gentler handling. Mixing these fabrics can lead to damage, so keep them separate. Before tossing anything into the wash, check for stains. Treat them with a stain remover or a bit of detergent, and let it sit for a few minutes. This pre-treatment can make a world of difference in getting those stubborn spots out.

Understanding laundry care labels is like deciphering a secret code, but it's essential for keeping your clothes in good condition. Below are some common symbols to look out for. Ignoring these can wreak havoc on your wardrobe.

1. **Tub with water**: Machine wash

- Number inside tub: Maximum temperature (in Celsius or Fahrenheit)

- Hand in tub: Hand wash only

- Tub with X: Do not wash

- Tub with a line underneath: Gentle cycle

- Tub with two lines underneath: Very gentle cycle (delicate fabrics)

2. **Triangle**: Can use any bleach

- Triangle with two lines inside: Only use non-chlorine bleach

- Triangle with X: Do not bleach

3. **Square with a circle inside**: Tumble dry

- Dot(s) inside the circle: Low (1 dot), medium (2 dots), or high (3 dots) heat

4. **Circle with X**: Do not tumble dry

- Square with a curved line at the top: Line dry

- Square with a horizontal line: Dry flat

- Square with diagonal lines in the corner: Dry in the shade

5. **Iron**: Can iron

- Dot(s) inside the iron: Low (1 dot), medium (2 dots), or high (3 dots) heat

- Iron with X: Do not iron

6. **Circle**: Dry clean

  - Letter inside the circle (P or F): Type of solvent for dry cleaning

  - Circle with X: Do not dry clean

  - Circle with W: Wet clean

  - Circle with X: Do not wet clean

Efficient washing and drying can save you time and extend the life of your clothes. Use the correct amount of detergent—more isn't always better. Too much can leave residue, making clothes feel stiff and irritating your skin. Select the correct wash cycle for the load. Heavy-duty for towels, delicate for, well, delicates. Avoid overloading the washing machine. Over-stuffing can prevent proper cleaning and increase wear and tear on your clothes.

Once washed, the way you dry your clothes matters. Shake out items before placing them in the dryer to reduce wrinkles. Consider air-drying delicates and items prone to shrinking. If using a dryer, don't forget to clean the lint trap after each load to improve efficiency and reduce fire hazards.

Folding and storing clothes properly can keep them in good shape and make your space look tidy. For t-shirts, the classic fold involves laying the shirt flat, folding in the sides, and then folding in half or thirds. Jeans can be folded by laying them flat, folding them in half lengthwise, and then folding them in thirds. Sweaters are best folded to avoid stretching, especially around the shoulders. Drawer organizers and dividers can be helpful, keeping everything in its place and easy to find.

Deciding between hanging and folding can depend on the item. Hang clothes that wrinkle easily, like shirts and dresses, using sturdy hangers to maintain their shape. Fold items like jeans, sweaters, and T-shirts to save space and prevent hanger marks. For smaller items like socks and underwear, drawer dividers keep things organized and accessible.

Keeping up with laundry might not be the most thrilling part of adulting, but mastering these skills can save you time, money, and the heartache of ruined clothes. So next time you're faced with a mountain of laundry, you'll know exactly what to do.

Basic Home Repairs: Fixing Leaks, Changing Lightbulbs, and More

It's Friday night, you're chilling on the couch, binge-watching your favorite show, when suddenly, you hear a drip... drip... drip. Your sink has decided to audition for a horror movie, and now you're faced with the dreaded task of fixing it. But hold up, learning basic home repair skills is not just about avoiding the cost of a plumber. It's about becoming more self-sufficient and confident. When you know how to tackle minor repairs, you prevent small problems from snowballing into bigger, more expensive issues. Plus, there's an undeniable satisfaction in knowing you can handle your home's quirks without calling for backup.

First things first, let's talk tools. Having a basic toolkit handy is priority.

- A **hammer** is your go-to for driving nails and disassembling things that need fixing.

- **Screwdrivers**, both flat-head and Phillips, are useful for many tasks, from tightening loose screws to assembling furniture.

- **Pliers** are great for gripping, bending, and cutting wires.

- **Wrenches**, especially adjustable ones, are fundamental for tightening and loosening bolts and nuts.

- A **plunger** and a **plumber's snake** are lifesavers for unclogging drains.

- A **tape measure** ensures you're precise in your repairs, while a **level** helps you hang things straight.

- A **utility knife** is versatile for cutting materials and opening all those Amazon deliveries.

Having these tools on hand means you're ready for most common household repairs.

Let's dive into some step-by-step guides for common home repairs.

Fixing a leaky faucet might seem daunting, but it's manageable.

1. Start by turning off the water supply to the faucet. These are knobs found under the sink. *If you skip this step, you will create a geyser in your kitchen or bathroom.*

2. Then, remove the handle using a screwdriver.

3. Once you have access to the valve, replace the washer or O-ring,

which is usually the culprit for leaks.

4. Reassemble the faucet, turn the water back on, and test for leaks.

Voilà, no more drip-drip-drip haunting your dreams.

Unclogging a drain (or toilet) is another skill that will save you from many a frustrating morning.

1. Begin with a plunger to create suction and dislodge the clog.

2. If that doesn't work, use a plumber's snake. Insert the snake into the drain and twist it to break up the blockage.

3. Pull the snake out and run hot water to clear any remaining debris.

Your drain should now flow smoothly. Knowing how to tackle these issues can save you the inconvenience and cost of calling a plumber.

Patching small holes in walls is a handy skill, especially if you're renting and want to avoid losing your security deposit.

1. Start by cleaning the area around the hole.

2. Apply a small amount of spackle or wall filler with a putty knife, smoothing it over the hole.

3. Let it dry, then sand it down until it's flush with the wall, and it's like the hole was never there.

This simple fix can make a big difference in the appearance of your home.

Replacing a light fixture sounds intimidating, but it's surprisingly straightforward.

1. First, turn off the power at the circuit breaker to avoid any shocks.

2. Remove the old fixture by unscrewing it from the ceiling and disconnecting the wires.

3. Connect the wires of the new fixture to the corresponding wires in the ceiling—black to black, white to white, and ground to ground.

4. Secure the new fixture in place, turn the power back on, and test it.

A new light fixture can instantly change the look of a room.

While basic home repairs are within reach, knowing when to call a professional is key. Electrical work beyond changing a fixture, like rewiring or circuit breaker issues, should be left to an electrician. Complex plumbing problems, such as mainline clogs or pipe replacements, require a plumber's expertise. Recognizing your limits and calling in the experts when necessary can save you from costly and potentially dangerous mistakes.

Organizing Small Spaces: Maximizing Efficiency and Comfort

Living in small spaces presents unique challenges that can often leave you feeling cramped or overwhelmed. Limited storage options mean you need to get creative to fit all your belongings. Clutter can pile up quickly, making your space feel even smaller and more chaotic. But fear not; there are ways to turn your tiny abode into a cozy, efficient haven.

One of the most effective ways to maximize storage in a small space is by utilizing vertical space. Think of your walls as untapped real estate. Install shelves and hooks to store items off the floor. Floating shelves can hold books, plants, and decor, while hooks can keep your bags and jackets organized. These free up floor space and add a decorative element to your room. Investing in multi-functional furniture is a great way to save space. Storage ottomans, for instance, can serve as both seating and a great place to stash blankets or books. Loft beds can open up valuable floor space underneath for a desk or seating area. Under-bed storage containers are also a lifesaver for stowing away seasonal clothes or extra linens.

Decluttering is imperative for maintaining an organized home, especially in small spaces. The "one in, one out" rule is a simple yet effective strategy. For every new item you bring in, get rid of one you no longer need. This prevents your space from becoming overcrowded. Regularly purging items is also essential. Set aside time every few months to go through your belongings and donate or discard anything that no longer serves you. Organizing by category can make this process more manageable. Focus on one category at a time, such as clothes, books, or kitchen items, and sort through them thoroughly. This method helps you see exactly what you have and what you can let go of.

Creating comfortable and functional living areas in a small space requires thoughtful arrangement and personal touches. Start by arranging your furniture for optimal flow and space. Place larger pieces against the walls to open up the center of the room. Use furniture that serves multiple purposes, like a dining table that doubles as a workspace. Mirrors are a fantastic tool for making a small space feel larger. They reflect light and create the illusion of more space. Position a large mirror opposite a window to maximize natural light and make the room feel airier. Adding personal touches with decor and lighting can transform your space from a cramped area to a cozy retreat. Use soft lighting to create a warm atmosphere. Fairy lights, floor lamps, and table lamps can add ambiance without taking up much space. Decorate with items that make you happy, like artwork, plants, and meaningful trinkets. Personal touches make your space feel like home and reflect your personality.

Living in a small space doesn't mean you have to sacrifice comfort or style. Implementing these strategies can help create a functional, organized, and cozy living environment that makes the most of every square inch.

Sustainable Living: Eco-Friendly Household Practices

Adopting eco-friendly practices isn't just about saving the planet—it's also about taking care of yourself and your wallet. Sustainable living reduces your carbon footprint, which means you're helping to combat climate change. By making small changes, you contribute to a larger impact. Plus, eco-friendly practices often lead to lower energy and water bills, which save you money in the long run. And let's not forget that creating a healthier living space is a huge benefit. Fewer chemicals and pollutants in your home mean better air quality and overall well-being.

Reducing household waste is a great starting point. Composting organic waste is an easy way to minimize what you send to the landfill. Food scraps, coffee grounds, and even paper towels can be composted. This reduces waste and creates nutrient-rich soil for your plants. Recycling properly is another critical step. Make sure to rinse out containers and sort your recyclables correctly to avoid contamination. Using reusable items like cloth bags, stainless-steel straws, and glass containers can significantly cut down on single-use plastics. Every little bit helps!

Conserving energy and water is another impactful area. Start by installing energy-efficient light bulbs. LED bulbs use less energy and last longer than traditional incandescent bulbs. Using water-saving devices like low-flow shower heads and faucet aerators can reduce water consumption without sacrificing performance. Unplugging electronics when not in use might seem minor, but it adds up. Many devices draw power even when turned off, a phenomenon known as "phantom load." Using power strips makes it easier to disconnect multiple devices at once. These changes don't just save resources; they also lower your utility bills.

Choosing eco-friendly products can further enhance your sustainable lifestyle. Vinegar and baking soda, natural cleaning products, are effective and non-toxic alternatives to chemical-laden cleaners. They can tackle everything from countertops to bathroom tiles without harming your health or the environment. Supporting brands with sustainable practices is another way to make a difference. Look for companies that prioritize eco-friendly packaging, ethical sourcing, and fair labor practices. Your purchasing choices can drive demand for more sustainable products.

Checklist: Steps to Sustainable Living

1. Compost organic waste.

2. Recycle properly.

3. Use reusable items (cloth bags, stainless-steel straws, glass containers).

4. Install energy-efficient light bulbs.

5. Use water-saving devices (low-flow shower heads, faucet aerators).

6. Unplug electronics when not in use.

7. Choose natural cleaning products (vinegar, baking soda).

8. Support brands with sustainable practices.

Sustainable living is about making conscious choices that benefit both you and the environment. It's not about being perfect but about making small, consistent changes that add up over time. Adopting these practices helps to create a healthier home, save money, and contribute to a more sustainable future.

Key takeaways:

1. Establishing a regular cleaning routine and staying organized can greatly impact your mental well-being and productivity.

2. Learning to handle laundry, including treating stains, can extend the life of your clothes.

3. Basic home repairs are a valuable skill, saving you time and money.

4. Efficient organization of your living space can make daily tasks more manageable and less time-consuming.

Chapter 9

Navigating the Healthcare System

I magine you're out with friends, trying to enjoy a nice evening, when you suddenly feel a strange pain in your side. You try to shake it off, but it doesn't go away. The next day, you're in the emergency room, and the doctor hands you a bill that makes your jaw drop. This is where having health insurance comes in, acting like a trusty sidekick in the often confusing world of healthcare. Let's break it down so you can understand why this sidekick is so important and how to choose the right one for you.

Choosing Health Insurance: Understanding Your Options

Health insurance is essential for both financial and health protection. Without it, medical expenses can pile up faster than you can say "co-pay." Let's say you need an MRI, and you don't have insurance. That one scan could set you back over $2,000. Or consider a more serious situation, like needing surgery, which can cost tens of thousands of dollars. According to a study, nearly one in five uninsured adults in the U.S. went without necessary medical care due to cost. Health insurance helps you avoid these sky-high expenses by covering a significant portion of your medical bills. It turns those jaw-dropping numbers into manageable ones, allowing you to focus on your health rather than your wallet.

There are several types of health insurance plans to choose from. Employer-sponsored insurance is one of the most common types and is offered by many companies as part of their benefits package. These plans often come with lower premiums because your employer pays part of the cost. Individual plans from the marketplace are another option. You can purchase these plans through the Health Insurance Marketplace, where you might qualify for subsidies to help lower your costs. Government programs like Medicaid and Medicare are available for those who meet specific criteria. Medicaid provides coverage for low-income individuals and families, while Medicare is primarily for those aged 65 and older or with certain disabilities.

Health Maintenance Organizations (HMOs) and Preferred Provider Organizations (PPOs) are two common types of plans you'll encounter. HMOs generally require you to choose a primary care physician (PCP) and obtain referrals to see specialists. They often have lower premiums but less flexibility in choosing providers. PPOs, however, offer more flexibility, allowing you to see any healthcare provider without a referral. However, they usually come with higher premiums. Understanding your options helps you make an informed decision about which type of plan fits your needs best.

When diving into health insurance, you'll come across some terms and concepts that might initially seem like a foreign language.

- **Premiums** are the monthly payments you make to keep your insurance active.

- **Deductible** is the amount you pay out-of-pocket before your insurance starts covering expenses.

- **Co-pays** are fixed amounts you pay for specific services, like a doctor's visit.

- **In-network providers** have agreements with your insurance company to offer services at reduced rates.

- **Out-of-network providers** do not, often resulting in higher costs for you.

- The **Explanation of Benefits (EOB)** is a statement from your insurance company detailing what they covered and what you owe after a medical visit.

- **Health Savings Accounts (HSA)** and **Flexible Spending Accounts (FSA)** are special savings accounts that allow you to save pre-tax money for medical expenses, providing tax benefits and helping you manage healthcare costs more effectively.

Choosing the right health insurance plan involves assessing personal and family healthcare needs. Consider how often you visit the doctor, if you need regular prescriptions, or if you have any ongoing health issues. Compare plan coverage and costs, looking at premiums, deductibles, co-pays, and out-of-pocket maximums. Check provider networks to see if your preferred doctors and hospitals are included. Examine prescription drug coverage to make sure your medications are covered at reasonable prices. Using online comparison tools can simplify this process, allowing you to compare multiple plans side-by-side and find the best fit for your needs and budget.

Enrolling in health insurance is the next step. If you work for a company that offers health insurance, you can usually sign up within 30–90 days of hire. Then, they will have an open enrollment period annually where you can confirm or change your selected plan. You can also use the Health Insurance Marketplace, a user-friendly online platform where you can compare and purchase individual plans. Open enrollment periods are specific times of the year when you can sign up for or change your health insurance plan. Missing this window usually means you have to wait until the next open enrollment period unless you qualify for a special enrollment circumstance, such as job loss, marriage, or having a baby. These special circumstances allow you to enroll outside the regular period, ensuring you don't go without coverage during significant life changes.

Navigating the healthcare system can feel like a maze, but understanding your health insurance options and how to choose the right plan turns that maze into a clear path. With this knowledge, you can confidently face any medical situation, knowing you're financially protected and have access to the care you need.

Making Doctor Appointments: What to Expect

Finding the proper healthcare provider can sometimes feel like searching for a needle in a haystack, but don't worry—I've got your back. The first step is to check provider credentials and reviews. Think of it like vetting a potential date on social media. You want to make sure they have the right qualifications and a good track record. Websites like *Healthgrades* and *ZocDoc* offer reviews from other patients, giving you a snapshot of what to expect. But don't stop there; ask your friends or family for recommendations. Personal experiences can provide valuable insights you won't find online.

Location and availability are convenient factors. You don't want to trek across town every time you need a checkup. Look for providers close to your home or workplace. Convenience can make a big difference, especially if you need frequent visits. Verify that the provider's office hours align with your schedule. Some providers offer evening or weekend appointments, which can be a lifesaver if you work a 9-to-5 job. Lastly, make sure the provider accepts your insurance. Nothing is worse than getting a hefty bill because your doctor is out-of-network. Call their office or check their website to confirm they take your plan.

When it comes to scheduling medical appointments, efficiency is key. Many healthcare providers now offer online scheduling platforms, allowing you to book appointments without making a phone call. This can be a real time-saver. If online scheduling isn't available, don't hesitate to contact the provider directly. Receptionists are usually more than happy to help you find a convenient time. Utilizing patient portals can also streamline the process. These online systems let you book appointments, view your medical history, and even message your doctor. It's like having a personal assistant for your healthcare needs.

Preparing for a medical appointment helps you get the most out of your visit. Start by gathering your medical records and history. This includes previous diagnoses, treatments, and any medications you're currently taking. Having this information handy guarantees your provider has a complete picture of your health. Next, prepare a list of questions and concerns. Think about what you want to discuss during your appointment. Whether it's a new symptom or a question about medication, writing it down helps you remember to bring it up. Bring necessary identification and insurance information, such as your ID and insurance card. Arriving early gives you time to complete any necessary paperwork without feeling rushed.

Communication with your healthcare provider is paramount. Describing your symptoms accurately helps your doctor make an accurate diagnosis. Be specific about what you're experiencing, including the duration and intensity of your symptoms. Discuss treatment options and preferences openly. Your provider can offer various treatment plans, but choosing one that aligns with your lifestyle and comfort level is up to you. Don't hesitate to ask for clarification if something isn't clear. Medical jargon can be confusing, and it's your right to understand your treatment fully.

Reflection Exercise: Preparing for Your Next Doctor's Appointment

1. Gather your medical records and history, including any recent lab results or imaging reports.

2. Write down all of the questions or concerns you want to discuss with your doctor.

3. Confirm your appointment time, location, and any necessary paperwork with the provider's office.

4. Arrive 10–15 minutes early to complete any required forms and settle in before your appointment.

By taking these steps, you can ensure a productive and stress-free visit to your healthcare provider.

Maintaining Overall Health: Regular Checkups and Preventative Care

Ever had that moment when you can't remember the last time you saw a doctor? You're not alone. But here's the thing—regular medical checkups are your secret weapon for staying ahead of health issues. It's like getting your car serviced regularly to avoid a breakdown. Routine visits assist in the early detection of health issues before they become big, expensive problems. Imagine catching high blood pressure early. It's manageable with lifestyle changes and medication. Ignore it, and you might be dealing with heart disease or stroke down the line.

Another step not to be overlooked is keeping vaccinations up to date. Vaccines protect you from various diseases, some of which can be quite severe. Remember that tetanus shot you got as a kid? It's not a one-and-done deal. Adults need boosters, too. Monitoring chronic conditions like diabetes or asthma helps keep them under control, preventing complications. Regular checkups also build a relationship with your healthcare provider. This relationship is invaluable because your doctor gets to know you and your health history, making it easier to spot changes or issues early on.

So, what health screenings and exams should you be getting? Blood pressure and cholesterol checks are a must. High blood pressure is often referred to as the "silent killer" because it has no symptoms but can lead to serious health problems. Regular checks can catch it early. Cholesterol levels are equally important. High cholesterol clogs your arteries, leading to heart disease. Diabetes screenings are necessary if you have risk factors like obesity or a family history. Don't forget dental exams. Your oral health can affect your overall health.

Staying on top of preventative care might seem like a lot to juggle, but some practical tips can make it manageable. Setting reminders for appointments is a simple yet effective strategy. Use your phone's calendar app to set reminders for yearly checkups or bi-annual dental visits. Discussing a preventative care plan with your doctor is also a good idea. They can help you prioritize which screenings and exams you need based on age, gender, and health history.

Adopting healthy lifestyle habits makes your preventative care a breeze. Eating a balanced diet fuels your body with the nutrients it needs to function optimally. Think of it as putting premium gas in your car; it just runs better. Engaging in regular physical activity is another key component. You don't have to become a gym rat, but incorporating activities like walking, swimming, or yoga into your routine can make a big difference. Getting adequate sleep is often overlooked but is vital for overall well-being. Aim for 7-9 hours of quality sleep each night. Managing stress effectively is the final piece of the puzzle. Chronic stress can take a serious toll on your body, leading to issues like high blood pressure, anxiety, and depression.

Meditation, deep breathing exercises, and even hobbies can help keep stress levels in check.

Regular medical checkups and preventative care are like having a safety net for your health. They catch issues early, keep chronic conditions in check, and build a relationship with your healthcare provider. By staying on top of recommended screenings and adopting healthy lifestyle habits, you set yourself up for a healthier, happier life. So, next time you think about skipping that annual checkup, remember that a little time invested now can save you lots of trouble later.

Basic First Aid: Handling Common Injuries and Illnesses

Imagine you're at a summer BBQ, and someone accidentally cuts their finger while slicing a watermelon. It's a small cut, but it starts bleeding, and everyone looks around for a hero. Knowing basic first aid can make you that hero, ready to provide immediate emergency assistance. Providing first aid can reduce the severity of injuries and stabilize conditions until professional help arrives. Immediate care can prevent a small injury from becoming a big problem; sometimes, it's the difference between a minor scare and a major emergency. Let's talk about handling some common injuries.

- **Cuts and scrapes**. When someone gets a cut, the first step is to clean the wound to prevent infection. Rinse it under running water and gently remove any debris with tweezers. Apply an antiseptic to kill bacteria, then cover the wound with a sterile bandage. It can also help to apply an antibiotic ointment like Neosporin. Keep an eye on it and change the bandage daily or whenever it gets wet. Follow the same steps for scrapes, but you might need a larger bandage or gauze pad to cover the area. It's simple, but it makes a huge difference in preventing infections and promoting healing.

- **Sprains and strains** are another common issue. You know that moment when you step off a curb wrong and twist your ankle? That's a sprain. The best way to manage it is with the RICE method: Rest, Ice, Compression, and Elevation. Rest the injured part as much as possible. Apply ice packs wrapped in a cloth for 20 minutes every hour to reduce swelling. Use an elastic bandage to compress the area, but not so tight that it cuts off circulation. Elevate the injured part above your heart level to minimize swelling. It's not rocket science, but it helps your body heal faster and reduces pain.

- **Burns** are another injury you might come across. Knowing how to handle burns is crucial, whether it's from a hot stove or a sunburn. For minor burns, run cool water over the area for at least 10 minutes. This helps reduce pain and swelling. Avoid using ice, as it may cause further damage to the skin. After cooling the burn, apply an aloe vera gel or a burn ointment to soothe the skin. Cover the burn with a loose, sterile bandage or clean cloth. For more severe burns, especially if blisters form or the skin looks charred, seek professional medical help immediately. Burns can be tricky, but quick and correct action can prevent complications.

- **Insect bites and stings** can be more than just annoying; they can be dangerous if you're allergic. If someone gets stung by a bee and shows signs of an allergic reaction such as swelling, difficulty breathing, or dizziness, use an epinephrine injector if available and call 911 immediately. For non-allergic reactions, remove the stinger if present by scraping it off with a credit card or fingernail. Avoid using tweezers, as they can squeeze more venom into the skin. Wash the area with soap and water, then apply an antiseptic.

Ice packs help reduce swelling and pain. Over-the-counter antihistamines can also relieve itching and swelling.

Recognizing and responding to medical emergencies can be a life-saving skill. Knowing the signs of a heart attack or stroke can save lives. Symptoms of a heart attack include chest pain, shortness of breath, nausea, and lightheadedness. If you suspect someone is having a heart attack, call 911 immediately and have them chew an aspirin if they're not allergic. For strokes, remember the acronym FAST: Face drooping, Arm weakness, Speech difficulty, and Time to call 911. These quick actions can mean the difference between life and death, so you must act fast.

Choking is another emergency that requires immediate action. If someone is choking and can't speak, cough, or breathe, perform the Heimlich maneuver. Stand behind the person, wrap your arms around their waist, and make a fist with one hand. Place the thumb side of your fist just above their belly button and grab it with your other hand. Perform quick, upward thrusts until the object is expelled. If the person becomes unconscious, call 911 and start CPR. Administering CPR involves chest compressions and rescue breaths to keep blood and oxygen flowing to vital organs until professional help arrives. It's a skill worth learning, as it can save a life in critical moments.

Having a well-stocked first aid kit is like having a Swiss Army knife for health emergencies. Your kit should include basic supplies like bandages, antiseptics, gauze pads, and adhesive tape. Include over-the-counter medications such as pain relievers, antihistamines, and hydrocortisone cream. Don't forget to add tweezers, scissors, and a digital thermometer. Keep a list of emergency contact numbers, including your doctor and local hospital, and make sure everyone in the house knows where the kit is located. Regularly check and replenish your kit so that it's always ready when you need it.

In conclusion, knowing basic first aid equips you with skills to handle common injuries and emergencies effectively. It's about being prepared and confident to act swiftly when the situation demands it. Your ability to provide immediate care can significantly impact the outcome of an injury or emergency, making you a reliable and valuable resource in any situation.

Key Takeaways:

1. Understanding how to choose the right health insurance for your needs is crucial.

2. Preparing for doctor appointments and maintaining regular checkups can help catch health issues early.

3. Knowing basic first aid and when to seek medical attention is essential for your safety and well-being.

Chapter 10
Travel and Safety Tips

Have you ever planned a trip, only to realize halfway through that you've blown your entire budget on overpriced tourist traps and fancy dinners? Traveling on a budget doesn't mean missing out on the fun stuff. In fact, it often means you get to experience a destination more authentically. Imagine being able to travel more frequently or extend your trips simply by being smarter with your money. This chapter is about helping you make the most of every dollar while exploring the world.

Budget Travel: Saving Money on Your Next Adventure

Traveling on a budget can transform your experience. For one, it allows you to travel more frequently. Instead of one big splurge, you can have multiple smaller trips. Would you rather spend one week in Paris or three weekends exploring different European cities? Budget travel also reduces financial stress. Nothing ruins a vacation faster than worrying about money. By saving where you can, you free up funds for things that matter—like that spontaneous parasailing adventure or an extra bottle of wine.

Finding affordable accommodations doesn't have to be a headache. Platforms like *Airbnb*, *Hostelworld*, and *Couchsurfing* offer budget-friendly choices that often come with unique perks. Airbnb lets you stay in a local's home, giving you an insider's view of the city. *Hostelworld* is great for meeting other travelers, and *Couchsurfing*—well, it's free, and you might make a lifelong friend. Budget hotels and motels are another option. They might not have the frills of a five-star resort, but they get the job done. And don't forget alternative accommodations like house sitting or camping. House sitting can be an incredible way to live like a local without the hefty price tag, and camping brings you closer to nature, often for just the cost of a campsite.

Transportation is another area where you can save big. Booking flights during sales and using fare comparison websites like *Skyscanner* can score you some seriously cheap tickets. Set up travel alerts to get notified of last-minute deals. Once you've arrived, ditch the taxis and embrace public transportation. It's cheaper, and you can observe daily life from a local's perspective. Services like *BlaBlaCar* have carpooling offers that are not only affordable but also eco-friendly. Renting a car and splitting the cost can be economical if you're traveling in a group.

Food and activities can quickly eat up your budget if you're not careful. Shopping at local markets and cooking your own meals can save a ton. Plus, you get to try your hand at cooking with local ingredients—a fun and educational experience. Look for free or low-cost attractions and activities. Many cities offer free walking tours; a fantastic way to learn about the history and culture. Museums often have free entry days or reduced prices for students. And don't underestimate the joy of exploring parks, beaches, and other public spaces. Using discount cards or tourist passes can also help. These often provide reduced rates or even free entry to multiple attractions.

Incorporating these strategies into your travel planning saves money and enriches your experience. Traveling on a budget encourages you to explore off the beaten path, interact with locals, and immerse yourself in the culture. It's about making smart choices that allow you to travel more, stress less, and create unforgettable memories. So, pack your bags, grab your travel buddy (or go solo), and get ready to see the world without breaking the bank.

Packing Like a Pro: What to Bring and What to Leave At Home

Packing for a trip can either be a breeze or a nightmare, depending on how you approach it. So you're standing over an open suitcase, clothes strewn everywhere, and you're wondering how you're supposed to fit your entire wardrobe into a single carry-on. Creating an efficient packing list tailored to your destination and activities is the key to packing like a pro. Start by categorizing your items: clothing, toiletries, electronics, and any other necessities. Consider the weather and cultural norms for your destination. If you're heading to a tropical beach, you won't need that bulky sweater. Prioritize important items to avoid overpacking. Do you really need five pairs of shoes for a weekend getaway? Probably not.

When it comes to packing techniques, maximizing luggage space is an art form. Rolling your clothes instead of folding them saves significant space and reduces wrinkles. Packing cubes and compression bags make a big difference. They help organize and compress your items to free up more room in your suitcase. Stuffing small items like socks or chargers into shoes is another clever trick to utilize every inch of space. These tips help you pack more efficiently and avoid the dreaded "sit-on-the-suitcase-to-close-it" move.

It's important to choose travel-friendly clothing and gear. Take layers that can be added or removed as needed. Lightweight and quick-dry fabrics are your best friends. They save space and make laundry a breeze if you need to wash clothes on the go. You'll be grateful with comfortable and sturdy footwear. Whether hiking up a mountain or strolling through city streets, your feet will thank you. Trust me, nothing ruins a trip faster than blisters or sore feet.

It's equally important to know what to leave behind. Excessive clothing and shoes are usually unnecessary and take up valuable space. Bring versatile pieces that can be mixed and matched. Full-size toiletries should also stay at home. Select travel-size bottles or purchase toiletries at your destination. Not only does this save space and weight, but it also guarantees you comply with airport security regulations. Plus, it's a great excuse to try out local products.

Reflection Exercise: Packing Essentials and Non-Essentials

1. List all items you plan to pack.

2. Categorize them as must-have or nice-to-have.

3. Remove at least two items that are nice-to-have.

4. Re-evaluate your list for multipurpose items.

Following these guidelines, you can pack efficiently, save space, and bring only what you need. Whether you're heading on a short weekend trip or a month-long adventure, if you pack smart you'll have everything you need without the extra baggage. Enjoy your travels, knowing you've packed like a pro.

Navigating New Places: Travel Apps and Tools

You've just landed in a new city, your phone buzzes, and up pops a notification with real-time updates on how to get to your hostel, the best local eateries, and even a walking tour starting in an hour. Sounds like magic, right? Welcome to the world of travel apps, where technology turns your adventure into a seamless experience. Using travel apps can simplify your journey in ways you never thought possible. They offer convenience and real-time updates and enhance your safety and ease of navigation. No more fumbling with paper maps or struggling to communicate in a foreign language.

Navigation apps like *Google Maps* and *Citymapper* are lifesavers when it comes to finding your way around. *Google Maps* offers comprehensive directions whether you're walking, driving, or using public transport. It even shows real-time traffic updates and alternative routes to avoid delays. *Citymapper* is fantastic for navigating urban areas and providing detailed public transport information, including subway, bus, and bike routes. These apps help you explore confidently without getting lost.

Language barriers can be a major hurdle, but language translation apps like *Google Translate* and *Duolingo* make communication a breeze. *Google Translate* can translate text, voice, and even images instantly. Just snap a picture of a menu or a sign, and voilà, it's in your language. *Duolingo* is great if you want to learn some basics before your trip. It makes learning fun and interactive, helping you pick up everyday phrases that can enrich your travel experience.

Managing money in a foreign land can be tricky, but currency conversion apps like *XE Currency* have got you covered. *XE Currency* provides real-time exchange rates and allows you to track multiple currencies at once. This app works offline, too, so you always know exactly how much you're spending, even without an internet connection. No more guessing if you're getting a good deal or being ripped off.

Planning and booking your trip has never been easier with apps like *Skyscanner* and *Booking.com*. *Skyscanner* searches millions of flights to find the best ones, including filters for budget airlines and direct flights. *Booking.com* offers a vast selection of accommodations, from hotels to hostels and vacation rentals. These apps provide user reviews, photos, and detailed descriptions, helping you make informed decisions. And let's not forget about *TripAdvisor* and *Yelp* for finding local attractions and restaurants. These apps offer reviews, ratings, and tips from fellow travelers, so you don't miss out on hidden gems.

Staying connected while traveling is a must, and using local SIM cards or international data plans can save you from exorbitant roaming charges. Local SIM cards are often affordable and provide ample data for your needs. Alternatively, international data plans can be convenient for hopping between countries. Finding and connecting to Wi-Fi hotspots is another great way to stay online. Apps like *WiFi Map* help you locate nearby free Wi-Fi spots, so you're never out of touch.

Messaging apps like *WhatsApp* and *Viber* are great for maintaining communication with family and friends back home. They offer free text, voice, and video calls over Wi-Fi or data, keeping you connected without the hefty international call charges. These apps are also great for staying in touch with fellow travelers you meet along the way.

Incorporating travel apps into your journey enhances your experience by providing convenience, safety, and real-time information. They allow you to confidently navigate new places, communicate effortlessly, manage your money wisely, and stay connected easily. So, download these apps before your next adventure and let technology be your travel buddy.

Travel Safety: Staying Safe on the Road

When planning a trip, safety should be right up there with choosing your next Instagram-worthy destination. Start by researching your destination's safety. Check travel advisories from official sources like the U.S. State Department. These advisories give you the lowdown on potential risks, from political unrest to natural disasters. But don't stop there. Dive into traveler reviews and forums. Sites like *TripAdvisor* and *Reddit* can offer firsthand accounts of what to expect. Understanding local customs and laws is also good practice. What's perfectly acceptable behavior at home might be a big no-no abroad. Knowing these can save you from awkward or even dangerous situations.

Personal safety tips are your best friend when you're on the road. Keep your valuables secure by using money belts or anti-theft bags. These nifty items make it harder for pickpockets to get their hands on your stuff. Avoid risky areas, especially at night. This isn't about being paranoid, just smart. Stick to well-lit, populated areas and always use reputable transportation services. Whether it's a taxi, ride-share, or public transport, make sure it's legit. Always stay aware of your surroundings. It's easy to get lost in the beauty of a new place, but keeping an eye on what's happening around you can prevent many problems.

Health and safety precautions are another layer of protection. Get necessary vaccinations and medications before you go. Check with your doctor or a travel clinic to see what's recommended for your destination. Drink bottled or purified water to avoid any nasty surprises from the local tap water. Using sunscreen and insect repellent can save you from painful sunburns and itchy bites. Trust me, you don't want to spend your vacation scratching or nursing a burn.

Dealing with travel emergencies can be overwhelming, but a little preparation goes a long way. If you lose something important or it gets stolen, report it to local authorities immediately. Having a police report can be critical for insurance claims. Know where your local embassy or consulate is and how to contact them. They can help with everything from replacing lost passports to offering advice in a crisis. Accessing emergency medical care is also something to keep in mind. Know the local emergency numbers and, if possible, the locations of nearby hospitals or clinics.

Preparing for emergencies before you even leave home can save a lot of headaches. Make copies of important documents like your passport, insurance, and itinerary. Keep one set with you and leave another with someone you trust back home. Register your travel plans with your local embassy. You can do this online, then they can reach you in case of an emergency. Creating an emergency contact list is also a good idea. Include local emergency numbers, your embassy's contact information, and contacts back home. Keep this list in both digital and hard copy forms.

Taking these steps might sound like a lot of work, but they're worth it for the peace of mind they bring. Being prepared means you can focus on enjoying your trip, making memories, and maybe even learning a thing or two about the world and yourself. Go ahead and explore with confidence, knowing you've got the safety aspect covered.

Understanding Travel Insurance: What You Need to Know

You're hiking the stunning trails of the Swiss Alps, breathing in the crisp mountain air, when suddenly you trip and twist your ankle. Ouch! Now, instead of enjoying the view, you're worried about medical bills and how this unexpected incident will cut your trip short. This is where travel insurance steps in as your safety net. It's a crucial aspect of trip planning that many overlook, but it can save you from financial disaster. Travel insurance covers unexpected medical expenses, so you get the care you need without the hefty price tag. It also protects against trip cancellations and interruptions, so if your flight gets canceled or you need to cut your trip short due to an emergency, you won't be left out of pocket. And perhaps most importantly, it provides peace of mind. Knowing you're covered lets you enjoy your adventure without worrying about what-ifs.

There are different types of travel insurance, each tailored to cover specific needs. Medical insurance will help, especially if you're traveling abroad where your regular health insurance might not apply. This covers doctor visits, hospital stays, and even emergency dental work. Trip cancellation or interruption insurance reimburses you if unforeseen events—like a family emergency or natural disaster—force you to cancel or shorten your trip. If your luggage gets lost, stolen, or damaged, baggage and personal belongings insurance steps in. Imagine arriving in Paris only to find that your suitcase has decided to take its own vacation. This coverage helps replace your items so you can continue your trip. Lastly, emergency evacuation insurance covers the cost of getting you to the nearest adequate medical facility in case of a serious injury or illness. It's the kind of thing you hope you never need but will be incredibly grateful for if you do.

Choosing the right travel insurance policy can feel like a lot, but it doesn't have to. Start by comparing coverage options and exclusions. Not all policies are created equal, and some might not cover activities you plan to do, like scuba diving or skiing. Consider the length and nature of your trip. A week-long beach vacation might require different coverage than a month-long backpacking adventure through Asia. Reading reviews and getting recommendations from other travelers can also be incredibly helpful. Look for policies that have a track record of good customer service and hassle-free claims.

If something does go wrong and you need to file a travel insurance claim, the process is straightforward but requires diligence. Keep all documents and receipts related to your claim. This includes medical bills, police reports, and receipts for any expenses incurred due to the incident. Contact your insurance provider immediately to report the claim and follow their specific procedures. They might have forms for you to fill out or additional documentation requirements. Following these steps helps your claim get processed quickly and efficiently, getting you the reimbursement or support you need as soon as possible.

Incorporating travel insurance into your trip planning isn't about expecting the worst; it's about being prepared for anything. It's a precaution that lets you focus on the adventure, knowing you're covered if things go sideways. So, as you plan your next big trip, make sure travel insurance is on your checklist. It's a small investment for some peace of mind. With your travel safety sorted, it's time to think about the next step in your journey—making the most of your experiences and capturing those un-forgettable moments.

Key takeaways:

1. Traveling on a budget requires planning and research to find the best deals.

2. Packing efficiently can save you time, money, and stress.

3. Utilizing travel apps for bookings and local tips can enhance your travel experience.

4. Staying informed about travel insurance options can protect you from unforeseen circumstances.

Conclusion

Well, here we are at the end of our journey together. Remember those sweaty palms and racing heartbeats at the beginning of this book? Look at you now! You've tackled some of the most daunting aspects of adulting, and you're ready to face the world confidently. Let's take a quick stroll down memory lane and recap the main points we've covered.

First, we dove headfirst into mastering your finances. We talked about creating a realistic budget, building an emergency fund, understanding credit scores, managing debt, and dipping your toes into investing. You now know that budgeting isn't just a boring chore—it's the foundation for financial freedom.

Next, we navigated the job market. Crafting the perfect resume, acing interviews, negotiating job offers, and optimizing your LinkedIn profile are no longer mysteries to you. You're now armed with the tools to land that dream job and thrive in your career.

Time management and organization came next. You've learned how to turn chaos into order with techniques like the Pomodoro Technique, time blocking, and the Eisenhower Matrix. Planners, to-do lists, and digital tools are now your best friends in making the most of each day.

Prioritizing mental health and managing stress was another crucial area we tackled. Daily mindfulness practices, stress management strategies, overcoming anxiety, and building resilience are now part of your toolkit.

You understand that mental health is equally as important as physical health, if not more so.

Building strong relationships came next. Effective communication, conflict resolution, finding your support network, social media etiquette, and setting boundaries are now skills you've honed. You're ready to forge meaningful connections and maintain healthy relationships.

Moving out on your own was a big one. From finding the right place to live, choosing a roommate, and signing a lease, to handling basic home repairs, you're now prepared to take that leap into independence with confidence.

Cooking and nutrition skills were next on our list. You've learned about essential kitchen tools, meal planning, grocery shopping tips, and easy, healthy recipes. Your kitchen is no longer a place of fear but a playground for delicious and nutritious meals.

Managing a household might have seemed overwhelming at first, but no more! Cleaning routines, laundry tips, basic home repairs, and organizing small spaces are now second nature. You've also dipped your toes into sustainable living practices, making your home eco-friendly and efficient.

Navigating the healthcare system was another biggie. Choosing the right health insurance, making doctor appointments, maintaining overall health, and handling basic first aid are now skills you possess. You're ready to take charge of your health with confidence.

Finally, we covered travel and safety tips. Budget travel, packing like a pro, using travel apps, staying safe on the road, and understanding travel insurance are now part of your skill set. You're ready to explore the world without breaking the bank or compromising your safety.

The vision and purpose of this book have always been to provide you with the tools, strategies, and confidence to transition into adulthood smoothly and successfully. We wanted to shift your perspective from viewing adulting as an overwhelming monster to embracing it with a confident "I got this" mindset.

Now, it's time to take action. Apply the strategies and insights you've learned in this book to your own life. Start with small steps—create a budget, plan a meal, or set boundaries in your relationships. Remember, adulting is a journey, not a destination. You've got this!

With the right skills and knowledge, you can transition into adulthood confidently. The journey of adulting is ongoing, and it's okay to seek help to continue learning along the way. Embrace every challenge as an opportunity to grow and thrive.

Thank you for embarking on this journey with me. I hope this book has provided valuable insights and inspiration for your path to adulthood. Remember, you're not alone in this—many others are navigating the same journey, and together, we can support and uplift each other.

You've got the tools, the knowledge, and the confidence. Now go out there and show the world that you've got this, one adulting challenge at a time!

Keeping the Game Alive

You've made it! You've got the tools, the tips, and the know-how to master the Art of ADULTING. But before you head off to conquer the world (or at least your laundry pile), I have one last favor to ask.

Would you share your thoughts about this book?

Your honest review on Amazon could be the compass that helps other young adults find their way to the same life-changing knowledge. It's like passing the baton in a relay race—we keep the game alive by helping each other.

By taking just a minute to leave your review, you'll:

- Point others toward a resource that can change their lives.

- Help them realize that adulting isn't as scary as it seems.

- Inspire someone else to take the first step on their journey.

The Art of ADULTING thrives when we share what we've learned, and your review is a big part of that.

Thank you for being a part of this mission.

Click here to leave your review on Amazon: https://www.amazon.com/review/review-your-purchases/?asin=B0DWX3SBX6

Or scan this QR code:

Let's keep the Art of ADULTING alive—together!

Gratefully yours,
IRL Publishing
In. Real. Life.

References

Bank of America. (n.d.). *How to create a budget in 6 simple steps. Better Money Habits.* https://bettermoneyhabits.bankofamerica.com/en/saving-budgeting/creating-a-budget

Carrns, A. (2023). *The best budget apps for 2024. NerdWallet.* https://www.nerdwallet.com/article/finance/best-budget-apps

RBC Royal Bank. (n.d.). *The importance of having an emergency fund. Royal Bank of Canada.* https://www.rbcroyalbank.com/healthcare-financial-solutions/royal-college/advice-and-learning/article/?title=the-importance-of-having-an-emergency-fund-3-questions-answered

Consumer Financial Protection Bureau. (n.d.). *How do I get and keep a good credit score?* https://www.consumerfinance.gov/ask-cfpb/how-do-i-get-and-keep-a-good-credit-score-en-318/

Indeed. (2023). *Example resume for a young professional. Indeed Career Guide.* https://www.indeed.com/career-advice/resumes-cover-letters/resume-young-professional

Indeed. (2023). *Common interview questions for entry-level positions. Indeed Career Guide.* https://www.indeed.com/career-advice/interviewing/entry-level-interview-questions

Blanding, M. (2022, July 12). *How to negotiate your starting salary. Harvard Business Review.* https://hbr.org/2022/07/how-to-negotiate-your-starting-salary

NovoResume. (2023). 21+ essential LinkedIn profile tips for job-seekers. https://novoresume.com/career-blog/linkedin-profile-tips

University of Georgia. (n.d.). 10 strategies for better time management. UGA Extension. https://extension.uga.edu/publications/detail.html?number=C1042 &title=time-management-10-strategies-for-better-time-management

Clockwise. (2022). How to use Google Calendar for time management. https://www.getclockwise.com/blog/google-calendar-time-management

PCMag. (2023). The best task management apps for 2024. https://www .pcmag.com/picks/the-best-task-management-apps

Half Half Home. (2023). 19 tips to improve work-life balance while working remotely. https://www.halfhalfhome.com/work/work-life-balance.html

National Institutes of Health. (2021, June). Mindfulness for your health. NIH News in Health. https://newsinhealth.nih.gov/2021/06/mindfulness-your-health#:~:text=St udies%20suggest%20that%20focusing%20on,help%20people%20cope%20wit h%20pain.

Scott, E. (2023). 18 effective stress relief strategies. Verywell Mind. https: //www.verywellmind.com/tips-to-reduce-stress-3145195

Hofmann, S. G., & Smits, J. A. J. (2015). Cognitive-behavioral therapy for anxiety disorders: An update on the empirical evidence. Dialogues in Clinical Neuroscience, 17(3), 337–346. https://www.ncbi.nlm.nih.gov/pm c/articles/PMC4610618/

Lyra Health. (2022). Bouncing back: 8 expert tips for building resilience. https://www.lyrahealth.com/blog/building-resilience/

Verywell Mind. (2023). Why communication in relationships is so important. https://www.verywellmind.com/communication-in-relationshi ps-why-it-matters-and-how-to-improve-5218269

Scott, E. (2023). 7 active listening techniques for better communication. Verywell Mind. https://www.verywellmind.com/what-is-active-listening-3 024343

HelpGuide. (2022). Conflict resolution skills. https://www.helpguide.org/relationships/communication/conflict-resolution-skills

University at Buffalo School of Social Work. (n.d.). Developing your support system. UB School of Social Work. https://socialwork.buffalo.edu/resources/self-care-starter-kit/additional-self-care-resources/developing-your-support-system.html#:~:text=Support%20GroupReferences-,Benefits%20of%20a%20Social%20Support%20System,and%20report%20higher%20well%2Dbeing.

U.S. News & World Report. (2023). The 25 best places for young professionals to live. https://realestate.usnews.com/real-estate/slideshows/best-places-to-live-in-the-us-for-young-professionals

Common. (2021). How to find a roommate: A complete guide. https://www.common.com/blog/2021/09/how-to-find-a-roommate/

SpeedLegal. (2021). Lease agreement essentials: What to look for before you sign. https://speedlegal.io/post/lease-agreement-essentials-what-to-look-for-before-you-sign

Moving.com. (2023). How to set up utilities in your new home. https://www.moving.com/tips/how-to-set-up-utilities-in-your-new-home/

Bon Appétit. (2021). 10 essential kitchen tools for beginner cooks. https://www.bonappetit.com/story/10-essential-kitchen-tools-beginner-cooks

Corewell Health. (2023). Health benefits of meal planning. Corewell Health Blog. https://www.beaumont.org/health-wellness/blogs/health-benefits-of-meal-planning

U.S. Food and Drug Administration. (2023). How to understand and use the nutrition facts label. https://www.fda.gov/food/nutrition-facts-label/how-understand-and-use-nutrition-facts-label

Eatwell101. (2023). Healthy dinner recipes: 22 fast meals for busy nights. https://www.eatwell101.com/healthy-dinner-recipes-for-busy-nights

Wellbeing Magazine. (2023). The 5 key benefits of having a cleaning schedule. https://wellbeingmagazine.com/the-5-key-benefits-of-having-a-cleaning-schedule/

Stewart, M. (2022). *How to sort laundry for cleaner, fresher garments.* Martha Stewart. https://www.marthastewart.com/how-to-sort-laundry-86 72713

Tool Japan. (2023). *The 10 must-have tools for home repair.* https://www.tooljapan.jp/en-gb/press/latest-news/latest-blogs/the-10 -must-have-tools-for-home-repair.html

Better Homes & Gardens. (2022). 18 creative storage ideas for small spaces to get organized. https://www.bhg.com/decorating/small-spaces/strategies/cr eative-storage-ideas-for-small-spaces/

Healthcare.gov. (n.d.). *Health care coverage options for young adults.* htt ps://www.healthcare.gov/young-adults/

Greater Good Health. (n.d.). *Things to consider when choosing a healthcare provider.* https://greatergoodhealth.com/patients/things-to-consider-w hen-choosing-a-healthcare-provider/

Feinberg School of Medicine. (2021, June 11). *Routine medical checkups have important health benefits. Northwestern Medicine News.* https://news.feinberg.northwestern.edu/2021/06/11/routine-medica l-checkups-have-important-health-benefits/

American Red Cross. (n.d.). *First aid steps.* https://www.redcross.org/tak e-a-class/first-aid/performing-first-aid/first-aid-steps

EVERKI. (2023). *How to travel on a budget: 17 ways to save money.* https://www.everki.com/us_en/everki-stories/travel-on-a-budget.html

Nomadic Matt. (2024). *The best travel apps of 2024 to help you travel better.* https://www.nomadicmatt.com/travel-blogs/best-new-travel-apps/

Solo Traveler. (2023). *Solo travel safety: 50+ proven tips to keep you safe.* https://solotravelerworld.com/travel-safety/

NerdWallet. (2024). *How to find the best travel insurance.* https://www. nerdwallet.com/article/travel/travel-insurance